MW01675180

LifeLight

"In Him was life, and that life was the light of men." John 1:4

Exodus, Part 2

The Lord Covenants and Tabernacles with His People

LEADERS GUIDE

CONCORDIA PUBLISHING HOUSE · SAINT LOUIS

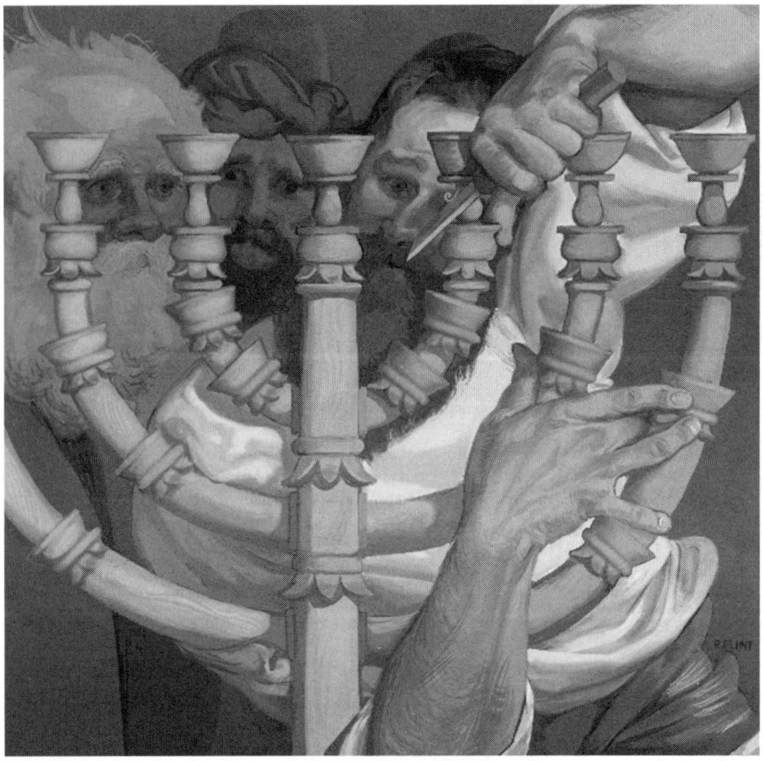

From the reed marshes along the Nile to the hardwood acacias in the Sinai Wilderness, the Lord guided His people. He guided the nimble fingers of Moses' mother, who wove a basket for her son. He strengthened the callous hands of Besalel and Oholiab, who gave shape to the tabernacle. And ultimately, with woven crown and splintered cross, He designed your Exodus, your salvation through Christ.

Earl H. Gaulke, editor

Revised from material prepared by Paul Raabe and Leland Stevens.

Denise Muhly and Lavern Schmidt, Field-Test Coordinators

Copyright © 1992, 2003 by Concordia Publishing House
3558 S. Jefferson Avenue
St. Louis, MO 63118-3968
Manufactured in the U.S.A.

This publication may be available in braille or large print or on cassette tape for the visually impaired. Please allow 8 to 12 weeks for delivery. Write to the Library for the Blind, 1333 S. Kirkwood Road, St. Louis, MO 63122-7295; call 1-800-433-3954, ext. 1322; or e-mail to blind.library@lcms.org.

All Scripture quotations, unless otherwise indicated, are from the HOLY BIBLE, NEW INTERNATIONAL VERSION®. NIV®. Copyright © 1973, 1978, 1984 by International Bible Society. Used by permission of Zondervan Publishing House. All rights reserved.

Scripture quotations marked RSV are from the Revised Standard Version of the Bible, copyright 1952 [2nd edition,1971], by the Division of Christian Education of the National Council of the Churches of Christ in the United States of America. Used by permission. All rights reserved.

The quotation from the Lutheran Confessions in this publication is from THE BOOK OF CONCORD: THE CONFESSIONS OF THE EVANGELICAL LUTHERAN CHURCH, edited by Theodore G. Tappert, copyright © 1959 Fortress Press. Used by permission of the publisher.

All rights reserved. No part of this publication may be reproduced, stored in a retrieval system, or transmitted, in any form or by any means, electronic, mechanical, photocopying, recording, or otherwise, without the prior written permission of Concordia Publishing House.

Cover illustration: © Russ Flint

1 2 3 4 5 6 7 8 9 10 12 11 10 09 08 07 06 05 04 03

Contents

Introduction

Welcome to LifeLight

A special pleasure is in store for you. You will be instrumental in leading your brothers and sisters in Christ closer to Him who is our life and light (John 1:4). You will have the pleasure of seeing fellow Christians discover new insights and rediscover old ones as they open the Scriptures and dig deep into them, perhaps deeper than they have ever dug before. More than that, you will have the pleasure of sharing in this wonderful study.

LifeLight—An In-depth Study

LifeLight is a series of in-depth Bible studies. The goal of LifeLight is that through a regular program of in-depth personal and group study of Scripture, more and more Christian adults may grow in their personal faith in Jesus Christ, enjoy fellowship with the members of His body, and reach out in love to others in witness and service.

In-depth means that this Bible study includes the following four components: individual daily home study; discussion in a small group; a lecture presentation on the Scripture portion under study; and an enhancement of the week's material (through reading the enrichment magazine).

LifeLight Participants

LifeLight participants are adults who desire a deeper study of the Scriptures than is available in the typical Sunday morning adult Bible class. (Mid-to-older teens might also be LifeLight participants.) While LifeLight does not assume an existing knowledge of the Bible or special experience or skills in Bible study, it does assume a level of commitment that will bring participants to each of the nine weekly assemblies having read the assigned readings and attempted to answer the study questions. Daily reading and study will require from 15 to 30 minutes for each of the five days preceding the LifeLight assembly. The day following the assembly will be spent reviewing the previous week's study by going over the completed study leaflet and the enrichment magazine.

LifeLight Leadership

While the in-depth process used by LifeLight begins with individual study and cannot achieve its aims without this individual effort, it cannot be completed by individual study alone. Therefore, trained leaders are necessary. You fill one or perhaps more of the important roles described below.

The Director

This person oversees the LifeLight program in a local center (which may be a congregation or a center operated by several neighboring congregations). The director

- serves as the parish LifeLight overall coordinator and leader;
- coordinates the scheduling of the LifeLight program;
- orders materials;
- convenes LifeLight leadership team meetings;
- develops publicity materials;
- recruits participants;
- maintains records and budgeting;
- assigns, with the leadership team, participants to small discussion groups;
- makes arrangements for facilities;
- communicates outreach opportunities to small-group leaders and to congregational boards;
- follows up on participants who leave the program.

The Assistant Director *(optional)*

This person may assist the director. Duties listed for the director may be assigned to the assistant director as mutually agreeable.

The Lecture Leader

This person prepares and delivers the lecture at the weekly assembly. **(Lesson material for the lecture leader begins on p. 9.)** The lecture leader

- prepares and presents the Bible study lecture to the large group;
- prepares worship activities (devotional thought, hymn, prayer) using resources in the study leaflet and leaders guide and possibly other outside sources;
- helps the small-group discussion leaders to grow in understanding the content of the lessons;
- encourages prayer at weekly leadership-team and discussion-leaders meetings.

The Small-Group Coordinator *(optional; the director may fill this role)*

This person supervises and coordinates the work of the small-group discussion leaders. The small-group coordinator

- recruits with the leadership team the small-group discussion leaders;
- trains or arranges for training of the discussion leaders;
- assists the director and discussion leaders in follow-up and outreach;
- encourages the discussion leaders to contact absent group members;
- participates in the weekly leadership-team and discussion-leaders equipping meetings;
- provides ongoing training and support as needed.

The Small-Group Discussion Leaders

These people guide and facilitate discussion of LifeLight participants in the small groups. **(Lesson material for the small-group leaders begins on p. 50.)** There should be one discussion leader for every group of no more than 12 participants. The small-group discussion leaders are, perhaps, those individuals who are most important to the success of the program. They should, therefore, be chosen with special care and be equipped with skills needed to guide discussion and to foster a caring fellowship within the group. These discussion leaders

- prepare each week for the small-group discussion by using the study leaflet and small-group leaders guide section for that session **(see p. 50)**;
- read the enrichment magazine as a study supplement;
- guide and facilitate discussion in their small group;
- encourage and assist the discussion group in prayer;
- foster fellowship and mutual care within the discussion group;
- attend weekly discussion leaders training meetings.

Leadership Training

LifeLight leaders will meet weekly to review the previous week's work and plan the coming week. At this session, leaders can address concerns and prepare for the coming session. LifeLight is a 1½-hour program with no possibility for it to be taught in the one hour typically available on Sunday mornings. Some congregations, however, may want to use the Sunday morning Bible study hour for LifeLight preparation and leadership training. In such a meeting, the lecture leader and/or small-group coordinator may lead the discussion leaders through the coming week's lesson, reserving 5 or 10 minutes for problem solving or other group concerns.

While it requires intense effort, LifeLight has proven to bring great benefit to LifeLight participants. The effort put into this program, both by leaders and by participants, will be rewarding and profitable.

The LifeLight Weekly Schedule

Here is how LifeLight will work week by week:

1. Before session 1, each participant will receive the study leaflet for session 1 and the enrichment magazine for the course. The study leaflet contains worship resources (for use both in individual daily study and at the opening of the following week's assembly) and readings and study questions for five days. Challenge questions will lead those participants who have the time and desire a greater challenge into even deeper levels of study.
2. After the five days of individual study at home, participants will gather for a weekly assembly of all LifeLight participants. The assembly will begin with a brief period of worship (5 minutes). Participants will then join their assigned small discussion groups (of 12 or fewer, who will remain the same throughout the course), where they will go over the week's study questions together (55 minutes). Assembling

together once again, participants will listen to a lecture presentation on the readings they have studied in the previous week and discussed in their small groups (20 minutes). After the lecture presentation, the director or another leader will distribute the study leaflet for the following week. Closing announcements and other necessary business may take another five minutes before dismissal.

In some places some small groups will not join the weekly assembly because of scheduling or other reasons. Such groups may meet at another time and place (perhaps in the home of one of the small group's members). They will follow the same schedule, but they may use the cassette tape to listen to the week's lecture presentation. The discussion leader will obtain the tape and leaflets from the director. A cassette tape version of the lecture is available for purchase from CPH (see your catalog). Or a congregation may record the lecture given by the lecture leader at the weekly assembly and duplicate it for use by other groups meeting later in the week.

3. On the day following the assembly, participants will review the preceding week's work by rereading the study leaflet they completed (and that they perhaps supplemented or corrected during the discussion in their small group) and by reading appropriate articles in the enrichment magazine.

Then the LifeLight weekly study process will begin all over again!

Recommended Study Resources for Exodus 2

Cole, Robert A. *Exodus,* Tyndale Old Testament Commentary. Downers Grove, IL: InterVarsity, 1972. A popular and generally helpful treatment of the text.

Concordia Self-Study Bible, New International Version. St. Louis: Concordia Publishing House, 1986. Interpretive notes on each page form a running commentary on the text. The book includes cross-references, a 35,000-word concordance, full-color maps, charts, and time lines.

Davis, John J. *Moses and the Gods of Egypt: Studies in the Book of Exodus.* 2d edition. Grand Rapids, MI: Baker, 1986. A study of the text, with special reference to the first 12 chapters in the light of recent archaeological and historical studies, with special reference to Egyptian religious and political customs.

Keil, C. F. and F. Delitzsch. *Biblical Commentary on the Old Testament: Vols. 1 and 2: The Pentateuch.* Grand Rapids, MI: Eerdmans, 1975 reprint.

Roehrs, Walter R., and Martin H. Franzmann. *Concordia Self-Study Commentary.* St. Louis: Concordia Publishing House, 1979. This one-volume commentary on the Bible contains 950 pages and is tailored for lay use.

Wendland, Ernst A. *Exodus,* The People's Bible Commentary. St. Louis: Concordia Publishing House, 1992. A popularly written commentary, referring to the New International Version of the Bible. Contains personal application as well as historical background and explanations of the text.

Every Voice a Song Pipe Organ Accompaniment for 180 Hymns and Liturgy. St. Louis: Concordia Publishing House (order no. 99-1565). Use this music CD for worship hymn accompaniment.

The Ten Words of the Covenant

Exodus 20:1–20

Preparing for the Session

Central Focus

This introductory session ties Exodus, Part 2 with Exodus, Part 1 and discusses the ten words or commandments.

Objectives

That the participant will be led to

1. repent of failure to keep the Law of God;
2. believe in the forgiveness of sins in Christ Jesus;
3. rejoice in the deliverance from bondage the Lord has given;
4. willingly and gladly follow the instructions of God's Law as one who is empowered by the Spirit working through the Gospel.

Note for the small-group leaders: Lesson notes and other materials you will need begin on page 50.

For the Lecture Leader

You have a key role in the process. Your weekly presentation will sum up the study the individuals have done all week at home and in small-group discussion. Because your part is important, you will want to prepare carefully each week.

Step 1 in your preparation: Pray for the Holy Spirit's guidance and illumination as you study and present God's Word. This is God's powerful and life-giving Word. It produces repentance and faith so that everything does not depend on your own abilities. That fact makes your work a joyful experience and not a burden.

Step 2: Read and study Exodus 20:1–20 for yourself. Only as the Word produces repentance and faith in your heart can you call others to repentance and faith.

Step 3: Prepare and practice your presentation carefully. If possible, make your presentation in your own words, using the printed lecture as a guide to follow. Speak the way you speak, and make the presentation your own. It is important to keep eye contact with the people and not to read the text. That facilitates communication.

Step 4: Ask someone in the group to help you by watching and listening to you carefully and then by giving you feedback. Pick someone who will be a positive and helpful critic.

Step 5: Pray again. Thank God for giving you an opportunity to declare His glorious name before others, and pray for His blessing.

For the Director

Before the first assembly confer with the presenter and discussion leaders about specific needs and the arrangement of meeting places.

The assembly area, where the opening worship, lecture, and closing activities take place, should be large enough for all participants to be seated comfortably. See that the area is heated or cooled, as well as ventilated, before the assembly is to begin. Arrange for a musician and instrument to accompany the hymn(s). (If a musician or instrument is not available and the entire group is not large, consider asking a congregation organist or a pianist to record the music on tape.) Ask the presenter how he or she prefers the audience to be seated (around tables, chairs in a circle or semicircle, chairs in rows, etc.). Does the presenter need a podium or lectern? a chalkboard? an overhead projector and screen? a chart stand or map? other items?

The areas where group discussions will take place must be ready also. Again, note heating/cooling and ventilation. How many chairs will be needed? Is a table desired? Are pencils on hand? Do the discussion leaders need special equipment? Discussion leaders will distribute study leaflet 1 at the beginning of the first assembly; arrange to have the needed number of leaflets available in the area where the beginning assembly takes place.

As the director you will also be responsible to see that any small groups meeting at a time other than the weekly assembly are supplied with the taped worship and lecture presentation (either recorded at the weekly assembly or using the cassette tape available with this course).

Session Plan

Worship

Begin the session with the hymn and prayer printed in the study leaflet. (Accompaniments are available in denominational hymnals, such as *Lutheran Worship* [refer to hymnal index]. Note: Concordia Publishing House has available *Every Voice a Song*, a 9-CD set of organ accompaniments for 180 hymns and liturgy. All the initial worship hymns in the LifeLight courses are included in this resource. It's especially helpful for mission congregations and small parishes. See the list of study resources on page 6.)

Lecture Presentation

Introduction

The subtitle of this LifeLight course is "The Lord Covenants and Tabernacles with His People." The Lord is the subject of the sentence and of the whole book of Exodus. Only when we concentrate our attention on the Lord, His words, and His deeds, rather than on ourselves, will we be able to understand Exodus.

"His people." Ancient Israel was not just an ordinary nation like the other nations. Israel was the Lord's people, called and delivered by the Lord. "His people" are the recipients of the divine action.

We, too, as the Lord's people and church in Christ, are the receivers of what God has done. Only when the Lord is seen as the actor and we as the recipients of that action do we rightly understand who we are.

The two verbs in the subtitle are also crucial. "The Lord *covenants* and *tabernacles* with His people." Our study together will flesh out these verbs and clarify them for you. Hopefully, by the end of our study you will see that these two powerful verbs provide a convenient summary of the Lord's actions in Exodus 20–40—and with us.

Exodus 20–40 consists of basically two parts. Chapters 20–24 concern the Lord's covenanting with Israel, and chapters 25–40 concern the Lord's tabernacling with Israel. This week we are focusing on the ten words of the covenant.

1 The God behind the Words (Exodus 20:1–2)

We know from Exodus 34:28 and Deuteronomy 4:13 and elsewhere that God gives Israel "ten words." But when Scripture gives us these ten words, they are not numbered, and so we cannot be certain exactly how they are to be numbered. It is not surprising, then, that different religions number them in different ways. Finally, how they are numbered does not matter, except for convenience in referring to them individually.

The text, in verse 1, refers to them as "these words." These words have a unique status. Only these words have a special name—"the ten words"—and they are repeated again in Deuteronomy 5. Only these words were spoken by God from Mount Sinai directly to the Israelites, without the mediation of Moses. After God spoke these words, the people trembled and asked Moses to serve as God's spokesman and mediator (vv. 18–19), which he did from then on. Only these words were written down on the two stone tablets (Deuteronomy 5:22). And a sense of finality sets the Decalogue (a common name for the commandments that means, literally, "ten words") apart from the remaining laws. Deuteronomy 5:22 says, "And He added nothing more." Therefore, these ten commands are special. In fact, most of the other laws are extensions, concrete applications, and clarifications of these ten. We rightly learn them well.

"These words" are statements of what we should and ought to do *and* what we *will* do. In other words, they are both prescriptions and descriptions of Israel's and of our behavior. They are both commandments of what God's people should do and predictions of what they will do. Therefore, they are called not only "commandments" but also "words."

Scripture refers to three purposes, or uses, that the Ten Commandments can have for people. For everyone, the Law serves as a *curb*; its threats curb and constrain human behavior. For example, when we drive, we don't speed lest we get caught and fined. Fear of punishment causes even thoughtless or careless people to obey. Laws prohibiting speeding are concerned with preserving and protecting human life; that is an application to the commandment "You shall not murder." That is the first use of the Law, to restrain behavior.

The second use or purpose of the Law is as a *mirror*. It

shows us our sins. It says, "You shall not covet" and causes us to realize that we *do* covet. By serving as a mirror, the Law sets us up and prepares us to receive the Gospel, the Good News concerning God's forgiveness of our sins for the sake of Jesus. The Law affects all people in these first two ways, because all people are sinners.

The third use or purpose of the Law, however, is only for believers, because only believers gladly want to obey their loving God. In this use the Law serves as a *guide.* It informs us how God would have us respond to His grace in Christ, and it describes how we, motivated by the Spirit, will—in fact—live. In other words, it describes the good fruit that a good tree will bear. However, because we Christians are still sinners, the Law also has to continue to function as a curb and mirror for us.

We can find these three uses or purposes of the Law in Exodus. The Law curbed Israel's disobedience when the Israelites saw the power of God and "trembled with fear" (v. 18). The Law as a mirror showed Israel its sin. This is why God later established the sacrificial system so that Israel might make atonement for their sins. If Israel would have been able to keep the Law, no sacrifices would have been necessary. Since Israelites were not only sinners but believers, the "ten words" (the Ten Commandments) guided, informed, and described to Israel how it would respond to its gracious Lord.

This brings us to the most important sentence in Exodus 20: "I am the LORD your God, who brought you out of Egypt, out of the land of slavery" (v. 2). This verse identifies the speaker. He is "the LORD." That is the way most of our Bible translations render the original Hebrew word *Yahweh.* Some translations use "Jehovah," but actually it is pronounced Yahweh (YAH-way). Thus, the original Hebrew reads, "I am Yahweh your God." The one speaking to Israel from Mount Sinai is Yahweh—that is His name. Notice that He reveals Himself as a *person,* with a personal name. God is not an "It," not an impersonal force. No, God is a personal being with a personal name, who speaks and acts as a person and who calls Israel (and us) into a personal relationship with Himself.

And this personal God who speaks here calls Himself "your God." He has graciously made Himself *your* God and has made you His people. He belongs to you, and you belong to Him. God spoke this way to ancient Israel, and He still speaks this way to us. The God of ancient Israel is our God, who has called us in Christ. Both the Old and New Testaments reveal the one and the same God.

The sentence continues: "who brought you out of Egypt, out of the land of slavery." The speaker continues to identify Himself by summarizing what He did—events recorded in the first 19 chapters of Exodus. So this sentence serves to bridge the first half of the book with the second half. Israel used to suffer in slavery to Egypt; it was forced to serve Pharaoh and his false gods by building their temples.

By grace, and not because of any merit or worthiness in Israel, Yahweh acted through Moses and delivered Israel from bondage and brought them to Himself into true freedom. As God said in Exodus 19:4: "You yourselves have seen what I did to Egypt, and how I carried you on eagles' wings and brought you to Myself." Israel did not deliver itself. The Israelites were helpless under Pharaoh's control in the land of slavery. But Yahweh defeated Pharaoh and the gods of Egypt (Exodus 12:12) and delivered helpless Israel.

The deliverance of ancient Israel from Egyptian slavery was a preview of the greater deliverance from sin, death, and the devil that we all have received by the work of Jesus Christ our Lord. God did the same saving act for us, only in a far greater way, that He did for ancient Israel.

In the following "words" God instructs and describes to ancient Israel (and to us) how they (and we) are to respond to His gracious and saving deed in Christ.

2 No Other Gods (Exodus 20:3–6)

The first "word" has three parts: the prohibition against other gods, the prohibition against images and idols, and the basis of these prohibitions. The first "word" begins, "You shall have no other gods before Me." The phrase "before Me" in the original Hebrew literally says "before (or upon) My face." Yahweh is not far away from Israel; He is in their midst. He made Himself their God and made them His people (v. 2).

Now He states the implications of this. His people will have only Yahweh as their God and no one or nothing else. In all that they say, think, and do, the God who delivered them and adopted them is to be their God and their only God. Israel should and will put no other gods before Yahweh's "face," that is, in His presence and before His eyes. Having other gods is never a secret or hidden thing. God is here with us, and He can see plainly what we do. To have other gods amounts to committing adultery and flaunting it right in the eyesight of one's spouse.

Verses 4–5 prohibit making an image or statue of God and then worshiping it. Why would this be wrong? Because Israel did not see God's appearance; they only heard Him speak and saw the cloud that enclosed Him (see Deuteronomy 4:11–24). Therefore, if they fashioned a statue of God, it would be based on their own imagination and reason. And certainly they should not worship such an image. That would be idolatry.

What is to prevent Israel and us from polytheism and idolatry? Two reasons are given in verses 5–6. First, because your God is a jealous God who punishes. It is not that He is at this time angry with Israel. He had recently delivered Israel by grace alone. He says, "I am Yahweh your God." He had, as it were, married Israel; He was the bridegroom, and Israel was His bride. But if His bride went after other "lovers," that would provoke Him to wrath. His "jealousy" is unlike human jealousy in that it is not fickle or irrational or selfish. But it is "jealousy" in the sense that He will not share His bride with other "lovers." If Israel goes after other gods or commits idolatry, that would provoke God to holy wrath and cause Him to punish "the children for the sin of the fathers to the third and fourth generation of those who hate Me" (v. 5). His punishment would not be unfair. He threatens to punish "those who hate Me." Nevertheless, all of Israel collectively, up to the fourth generation if they continued to hate Him, would suffer. Therefore, Israel was to fear God lest they provoke Him to wrath.

(20:6) Second, your God shows "love to a thousand generations of those who love Me and keep My commandments" (v. 6). God is not by nature angry or spiteful. The Old Testament repeatedly says that He is "the compassionate and gracious God, slow to anger, abounding in love and faithfulness" (Exodus 34:6). Notice that God's "love and faithfulness" outweighs His punishing wrath. God's anger extends to the fourth generation, but God's love and faithfulness extends to the thousandth generation (see Deuteronomy 7:9).

Those who benefit from this grace are those who love Him and keep His commandments. It is not *because* they love and obey Him; rather the sentence simply designates those who benefit, namely those who receive His grace and favor by faith alone, a faith that is active in love.

3 The Lord's Name (Exodus 20:7)

The next word prohibits misusing Yahweh's name. This refers to invoking God's name as a throwaway remark, not only in a negative way, such as cursing, but also in a neutral and meaningless way. God's name is holy and is to be treated as such. Again, notice the phrase "your God." You belong to Him, and He belongs to you. This relationship motivates you to love and honor His name. But there is also a threat (v. 7): "the LORD will not hold anyone guiltless who misuses His name." We do not want to provoke Him to anger. It is much like a cook's attitude toward a stove. The stove is a good and beneficial thing, but the cook also respects it so as not to get burned. In a similar way God's children do not trifle with God's name lest they anger Him. But more important, they love His name because it is the wonderful name of their loving Father.

4 The Sabbath (Exodus 20:8–11)

The third word is a positive one rather than a prohibition. Israel is to observe the Sabbath day as a day of rest and to keep it holy, that is, to set it apart from the other days of the week and dedicate it to their God. Why? Because God worked during the six days of creation but rested on the seventh day. Since Israel's God blessed and hallowed the seventh day, so should Israel. By observing the Sabbath day, Israel was sharing in God's sabbatical rest and was receiving a foretaste of the future heavenly rest that awaits God's people (see Hebrews 3–4).

Although we are no longer bound to worshiping on Saturday (Colossians 2:16), we, too, receive the blessings of God's rest and a foretaste of our future heavenly rest when we hear the Gospel, remember our Baptism, and partake of the Lord's Supper. Of course, we obey this commandment when we attend church on Sundays and at other opportunities and when we take part in Sunday school and Bible classes. But keeping this commandment involves far more than that. We also keep this commandment when we believe the Gospel that we hear and when we honor and uphold God's Word by living in a way that is in agreement with it and when our own attitudes toward others display the forgiveness, love, and consideration God has shown to us in Jesus.

5 Parents (Exodus 20:12)

The fourth word, like the third, is a positive one. It calls each individual Israelite to honor his or her father and mother. With what result? To this end (20:12): "You may live long in the land the LORD your God is giving you." The basic unit of Israel is the family. A strong and cohesive family will make for a strong and cohesive Israel in the Promised Land. So also with us. Strong Christian families help the church remain strong in the Lord, to the end that by God's grace we all together inherit the Promised Land where we will dwell forever—God's heavenly kingdom. Canaan, the literal Promised Land God would give to the Israelites, was a foretaste and preview of the new and greater Promised Land that awaits God's people, all those who are in Christ Jesus.

6 Life Together (Exodus 20:13–16)

The fifth through eighth words are all prohibitions. They set the boundaries of the Israelites' life together. The Israelites are not to murder, commit adultery, steal, nor bear false witness against their neighbor. These prohibitions also imply the positive. The Israelites should value and protect the gifts that God has given their neighbor, gifts such as life, spouse, property, and name. Out of faith and love toward the giver, we value the gifts our loving Father has given not only to us but also to our neighbor.

7 Coveting (Exodus 20:17)

The ninth and tenth words are also prohibitions. But notice how they address one's heart and not simply one's actions. They prohibit coveting: selfishly desiring anything of your neighbor's. God's will concerns both the inner motivation as well as external behavior. Again, the concern is that we, who have received from God blessings such as house, spouse, workers, and cattle for ourselves, value and protect the blessings God has also given our neighbor. The same God has blessed us and our neighbor with His creaturely gifts. To honor God is to protect the gifts He gave others as well as being good stewards of the gifts He gave us.

Conclusion

When we examine our lives in light of God's will, we can see only sin and disobedience. We confess with St. Paul, "For what I do is not the good I want to do; no, the evil I do not want to do—this I keep on doing" (Romans 7:19). And to us comes the Good News that "Christ redeemed us from the curse of the law by becoming a curse for us" (Galatians 3:13). We have been freed by Christ from an oppressive life under the Law. Just like ancient Israel we have been delivered from slavery and have been brought to God. We are now free to walk in the Law of God. As Ephesians 2:10 says, "For we are God's workmanship, created in Christ Jesus to do good works, which God prepared in advance for us to do."

The ten words show us our sin, but they also inform us of the good works in which we are called to walk in response to God's abundant steadfast love in Christ. Empowered by God's powerful Spirit working through the Gospel, we eagerly, happily, from a free and merry heart desire to walk in the Law of God. Why? Because the speaker is our God in Christ Jesus, who delivered us from the land of slavery.

Concluding Activities

Speak a brief prayer asking the Lord to bless this study and make any necessary announcements. Distribute study leaflet 2 and the enrichment magazine. Encourage participants to browse in the magazine and keep it as a helpful reference for coming lessons.

Encourage participants to set a weekly plan for their LifeLight study. A consistent daily schedule works best for most. Some begin or end the day with LifeLight. Others find another time during the day at home or during a break or lunch hour at work. Invite participants to share their practices, especially if your group has some who are new to LifeLight.

The Book of the Covenant

Exodus 20:21–23:33

Preparing for the Session

Central Focus

This session discusses the Book of the Covenant, a collection of the specific applications of the ten general "words" to the various dimensions of Israel's life.

Objectives

That the participant will be led to

1. repent of failure to keep the Law of God;
2. believe in the forgiveness of sins through the atoning sacrifice of Jesus Christ;
3. understand more clearly that God wills all of one's life to be in faith toward Him and fervent love toward one's neighbor;
4. willingly and gladly follow the instructions of God's will as one is empowered by the Spirit working through the Gospel.

Note for the small-group leaders: Lesson notes and other materials you will need begin on page 55.

For the Lecture Leader

Your major responsibility will continue to be the presentation of the lecture. Familiarize yourself thoroughly with the lecture so you will be able to present it effectively in your own style. If you read the lecture, practice reading it many times, so that you will be able to maintain eye contact with the listeners. Practice presenting the material with enthusiasm and excitement in an effort to make the material fresh and interesting.

The presenter might want to make an overhead that displays the outline of the lecture so that the people can follow along during the presentation.

Session Plan

Worship

Encourage participants to begin each day's study with prayer. Begin the session with the hymn and prayer printed in the study leaflet. (Accompaniments are available in denominational hymnals, such as *Lutheran Worship* [refer to hymnal index], or on the *Every Voice a Song* CD set.)

Lecture Presentation

Introduction

In the previous lesson we saw that God spoke the ten words from Mount Sinai directly and immediately to Israel. The people stood far from the mountain because of the thunder, lightning, and smoke that came from its top. We title this section "The Book of the Covenant" on the basis of Exodus 24:7. God spoke the following instructions to Moses on the mountain, and Moses was to relay them to Israel.

In these we find concrete and specific applications of the ten general words to the various dimensions of Israel's life. Exodus 21:1 calls them "laws." They do not exhaustively treat every possible situation, but they do illustrate how the ten words should be applied in various typical situations. Unlike the general statements of the ten words, many of the following judgments state the penalty for a given infraction. They are often expressed in a law form: "If so-and-so happens, then do this."

These judgments or ordinances were addressed to Israel. We saw in the last lesson that the ancient Israelites were God's people, an assembly called to faith in the true God. But ancient Israel was also a nation and a state. It was, in fact, a nation ruled by God, and so God revealed laws that were to regulate all aspects of life. Therefore, we find here civil laws as well as religious and moral laws all mixed together.

The church today, which the New Testament calls a new Israel (Galatians 6:16), is only a church and no longer a nation. So these civil laws no longer apply directly to us Christians. The church today does not, for example, exercise the power of punishment for civil crimes. Nevertheless, these laws are still worth studying. We should seek to determine what reason lies behind such laws. In many cases we will see that they are a practical application of one of the ten "words" or commandments.

1 Prologue (20:21–21:1)

The "laws" actually begin in 21:2. This opening section is a prologue. Through Moses God says to Israel, "You have seen for yourselves that I have spoken to you from heaven" (20:22). Then God prohibits Israel from making gods of silver or gold. Instead they are to make an altar for sacrifices.

We obtain several insights from this prologue. First, God is the source of the following laws. Israel is responsible to God and not to a human legislative body or lawgiver. Second, to disobey this law is to disobey God; it is sin and not simply an infraction of a secular law code. Finally, living in conformity with God's will flows from faith toward God. Just as the ten words began with the vertical dimension of Israel's relationship with God, so the following "laws" begin with this vertical dimension.

God repeats the prohibition against making idols. The logic is this: since you heard Me speaking, yet saw no visible form or representation, and since I am the God of heaven and not a created being, therefore give up any attempt to embody Me in a created image of silver or gold. Instead of through an image, God promises to meet Israel at an altar. That is where Israel will find God and receive God's blessing. "Wherever I cause My name to be honored, I will come to you and bless you" (v. 24). While wandering in the wilderness and in the early years in the Promised Land, the Israelites would want to know where they could find God and receive His blessing. Instead of contriving an image, Israel was to build an altar and offer sacrifices. At that place and through that means God promised to come to Israel and bless them.

The same applies to us. People want to know where to find God. They often invent their own devices for meeting God, devices that actually amount to idols. Instead, God has graciously made Himself accessible to us in those places where He has placed His saving name—in the Gospel, in Baptism, and in the Lord's Supper. Go to those places and receive His blessing there.

Notice that God would "bless" Israel. He promised to bless Israel through the animal sacrifices offered on legitimate altars. The animal sacrifices made atonement for Israel's sins. They did this by virtue of their connection with the all-sufficient sacrifice of Jesus Christ, which they foreshadowed and anticipated. In other words, the benefits of Christ's sacrifice were given to His Old Testament people through the animal sacrifices. The animal sacrifices offered on legitimate altars were Old Testament means of grace and blessing.

Israel's altars were to be made of earth or unhewn stones. To work the stone would "defile" the altar, that is, make it common and ordinary. The altar was to be distinct, because God is distinct, unique, and holy. Also, the priest's nakedness should not be exposed by climbing up steps to the altar. To expose one's nakedness publicly, which could happen if one wore a loose skirt or tunic and climbed steps, would be shameful, and such shamefulness is not appropriate to the holiness of God's altar.

2 Slavery (21:2–11)

The first group of "laws" concerns slaves. Slavery was common in the ancient world. But slavery in the Old Testament more closely approximated our own employer/employee relationships. An ancient "slave" was an indentured laborer and servant who lived with the owner's family. Since one's land could not be sold, as it was one's share of the Promised Land and was to remain with the family, the only collateral available to the Hebrews was their labor. To pay off their debts, Hebrews would sell themselves into indentured service. Yet aspects of this system were subject to abuse; therefore, God's Law spoke to these abuses. The law was intended to limit the control the master had over the servant.

In the seventh year, after six years of service, a male Hebrew slave was released and became a free man, without having to pay for the release. This is the "sabbatical year." Like the Sabbath day, the sabbatical year reflected God's resting on the seventh day of creation. If the master allowed the slave to marry one of the master's female slaves, probably a slave bound to the master permanently (Lev. 25:46), then the male slave either left single or voluntarily bound himself to the master for life.

The situation of the Hebrew slave-wife was different. She did not automatically go out in the seventh year, because her master-husband still had responsibilities toward her. Three critical situations might threaten her status. If she did not please her master, he had to allow her family to ransom her; he could not sell her to non-Israelites. If she was designated for the master's son, he had to treat her as a daughter. If the son took another wife (in the Old Testament God tolerated polygamy, though He did not endorse it), she had to be maintained with her full marital rights. In all of this the intent was to protect the slaves and uphold their human rights.

3 Capital Offenses (21:12–17)

The next set of laws concerns capital offenses. Human life is sacred, as people are created in the image of God (Genesis 9:6; James 3:9). Therefore, whoever assails human life forfeits his or her own life. Verse 12 states the basic principle, based on the commandment concerning killing: "Anyone who strikes a man and kills him shall surely be put to death." Verses 13–17 apply and clarify this general statement.

If the killing was unpremeditated, then the killer might seek asylum at an altar or in a city of refuge (Numbers 35:6). But there was to be no refuge for premeditated murder. That verses 13–14 distinguish between intentional and unintentional killing reveals that the life of the accused was also considered sacred. Kidnapping for slavery was common in the ancient world, but for Israel it was tantamount to attacking human life and not simply a crime against property. Verses 15 and 17 reinforce the commandment to honor parents. Not only striking but also cursing one's parents was a capital offense. To curse is to wholeheartedly will and pray for the downfall of the other; it is an attitude that leads to murder. Notice how the life of both parents was equally honored.

4 Bodily Injuries (21:18–32)

The five cases in this section deal with bodily injuries. Again, the concern is with people and the value they possess in God's eyes. The cases are a debilitating injury as a result of two men fighting in a sudden fit of rage (vv. 18–19), a master striking his slave (vv. 20–21), a woman's premature labor induced when hit by two men fighting (vv. 22–25), a permanent injury to a slave (vv. 26–27), and a goring ox (vv. 28–32).

In the first case (vv. 18–19), if the injured party was confined to bed and only later walked with the help of a cane, the assailant did not forfeit his life, but he had to pay the injured person for loss of time and income and care for him until recovery.

The second case (vv. 20–21) reveals that a master had no right to beat his slave to death deliberately, even if the master was legitimately chastising his slave with a rod. If the slave died immediately, that was proof enough that the master intentionally killed him, so the master should be punished, apparently by being put to death. But if the slave lived a day or two after the chastisement, that provided evidence that it was accidental homicide. In that case the financial loss incurred by his master in the death of the slave was considered punishment and lesson enough. Loss of the slave was a financial loss. Yet this law treated slaves as persons and not simply as money. It restricted the master's power over the slave.

For the third case (vv. 22–25), if a pregnant woman was accidentally struck and gave birth prematurely, but both mother and child were unharmed, the offender was fined. But if either mother or child was seriously injured, then the principle of "life for life" applied.

The principle "life for life, eye for eye, tooth for tooth," and so on was intended to restrict the punishment so that the punishment fit the crime but did not disproportionately exceed it. Verses 26–27 apply this principle to the situation of wounded slaves. They were set free. Again, this illustrates that slaves were to be treated as persons and not merely as property.

The final case (vv. 28–32) concerns injuries from animals. The goring ox was stoned, and its meat could be sold or eaten. The owner of the animal suffered a loss without any relieving profit.

5 Property Damage (21:33–22 15)

This section examines five types of property damage: punishable negligence (21:33–34), loss from animals fighting each other (21:35–36), loss from theft (22:1–4), losses from other negligent acts (22:5–6), and losses when goods are entrusted to another's custody (22:7–15). These cases apply the commandment concerning stealing to specific types of situations.

We can see several concerns in this section. First, property is not on the same value level as human life. Unlike capital offenses, the negligent offender or the thief did not forfeit his own life.

Second, the offending party had to make restitution for the damage done. If the thief had nothing, he became an indentured servant until he paid compensation. Third, the offending party made restitution directly to the party who suffered the loss. The restitution was not paid to a third party or a court to distribute. Even the thief had to conform to this direct restitution. No doubt this helped to promote reconciliation between the two parties. Finally, there is a concern for fairness. The reimbursement differed depending on the circumstances, and the cases distinguish between deliberate theft and inadvertent negligence.

6 Miscellaneous Stipulations (22:16–31)

This section consists of miscellaneous religious and social stipulations. The key statement that underscores the whole section comes in the last verse (v. 31): "You are to be My holy people." Israel was God's "treasured possession . . . a kingdom of priests and a holy nation" (19:5–6). 1 Peter 2:9 indicates that the New Testament church is the new Israel: "But you are a chosen people, a royal priesthood, a holy nation, a people belonging to God." To be a people "holy" to God means to have been consecrated and set apart unto the holy God. We were given this lofty status by being baptized in the name of this same triune God who speaks in the Old Testament.

Because Israel had this holy status, they were to lead a life worthy of their calling. That included worshiping Yahweh alone (vv. 18, 20, 28–30), honoring marriage (vv. 16–17, 19), and acting generously and compassionately toward the helpless, such as strangers, widows, orphans, and the poor (vv. 21–27). Notice the Gospel motivations given in this section. Just as God showed mercy to the Israelites, who were strangers in the land of Egypt, so they show mercy to strangers (v. 21). Because God hears the prayer of the widows, orphans, and the poor, Israel was not to afflict them (vv. 22–27). Because God is a compassionate God, Israel was to be compassionate also (v. 27).

7 Justice for All (23:1–9)

Where the previous section stressed compassion toward the helpless, this section exhorts Israel to be just. It expands on the commandment concerning false witness. The basis of justice lies in truth telling and impartiality. Therefore, the Israelites were not to slander (v. 1) or be partial toward anyone, either the poor (v. 3) or the rich (vv. 6, 8). Honesty, uprightness, and justice were to be the watchwords in Israel's courts. Even one's enemies were to be helped (vv. 4–5). The Old Testament never teaches us to hate our enemies. And what is the motivation for all of this? It is twofold: God is a just God who does not acquit the wicked (v. 7), and the Israelites knew from their experience in Egypt what it was like to be oppressed (v. 9).

8 Sabbaths and Holidays (23:10–19)

This section deals with Israel's agricultural-religious calendar. It is much like our church calendar in that it specifies certain festivals. This section basically expands on the commandment concerning the Sabbath. The Sabbath day was the day of the week that was set apart to God, much like a tithe of time. On this day Israel would hear the Word of God, receive the forgiveness of sins through the sacrifices, and respond in worship and praise to Yahweh alone (vv. 13, 18).

But the Sabbath day also served a humanitarian purpose. (Mark 2:27) "The Sabbath was made for man." It gave the Israelites, their servants, and even aliens and cattle a day of rest that they might "be refreshed" (v. 12). The Sabbath was also the basis of the Sabbatical year, when the land would rest and lie fallow. Obviously this was good for the land, but it also served to provide gleanings for the poor and for the wild animals (vv. 10–11). All of creation enjoyed a rest that anticipated the future rest of the new creation.

Verses 14–17 concern the three great festivals, when the Israelites in the Promised Land were to go on a pilgrimage to the sanctuary. The Feast of Unleavened Bread came in the spring and is associated with Passover. It commemorated that time when Israel hastily ate unleavened bread before the exodus from Egypt. The Feast of Harvest (sometimes called the Feast of Weeks or Pentecost) came seven weeks later. The Feast of Ingathering (sometimes called the Feast of Booths after the booths or tents Israel dwelt in during the wilderness wanderings) came in the fall, when the agricultural year ended. Each feast corresponded to a harvest activity, the first to the beginning of the barley harvest, the second to the wheat harvest, and the third to the harvest of grapes and olives. The firstfruits belong to God (v. 19).

9 Epilogue (23:20–33)

This last section serves as an epilogue to the Book of the Covenant. In it God promises to bring Israel safely into the Promised Land and exhorts them to remain faithful. Many of the previous laws addressed Israel's future life in the land, and here God promised an angel to bring them there. This is no ordinary angel, since Yahweh's "Name is in him," and He can forgive sins (v. 21). In light of the New Testament we can recognize Him as the pre-incarnate Christ.

God ends the Book of the Covenant where He began, with the First Commandment. The Israelites were to drive out the occupants of the land lest the Israelites make a covenant with them and worship their gods. Yahweh alone, working through His "angel," remains the center of Israel's life. We have seen how His will encompasses all aspects of the life of His people. Not only Sunday morning but every day and every activity centers in faith toward God and fervent love toward one another. So often we sin and are faithless. But God forgives us on the basis of the perfect sacrifice of Christ. He comes to us and blesses us through the Gospel and the Sacraments. And Christ goes before us and leads us through the wilderness to the Promised Land, a land flowing with milk and honey, a land where we will dwell with our God forever.

Closing Activities

Offer a brief prayer, thanking God for guiding us in our own lives through His Word. Make any necessary announcements. Ask whether participants are enjoying the enrichment magazine. Distribute study leaflet 3.

The Ratification of the Covenant

Exodus 24

Preparing for the Session

Central Focus

This session discusses the ratification of the covenant the Lord made with His people.

Objectives

That the participant will be led to

1. repent of sins, which make it impossible to stand before God on the basis of personal merit or worthiness;
2. grow in trust in the Lord Jesus Christ, who forgives us and shed His blood for all;
3. rejoice in the new covenant given through the shed blood of our Lord Jesus Christ;
4. appreciate more fully the wondrous gifts given in the Lord's Supper;
5. wholeheartedly say Amen to God's covenant with His people in Christ and gladly promise to lead a life worthy of his or her calling as one of God's people;
6. eagerly await the future coming of the Lord, when all will see Him face-to-face and believers will share in the messianic banquet.

Note for the small-group leaders: Lesson notes and other materials you will need begin on page 59.

For the Lecture Leader

Again, it might be helpful for the presenter to prepare an overhead visual aid that shows the outline of Exodus 24. This enables the participants to listen and follow along without having to read their Bibles at the same time.

Session Plan

Worship

Begin the session with the hymn printed in the study leaflet. (Accompaniments are available in denominational hymnals, such as *Lutheran Worship* [refer to hymnal index], or on the *Every Voice a Song* CD set.) Continue with the devotion below.

Devotion

A love for God's written Word characterized the Israelites. The longest psalm, Psalm 119, is an artfully constructed poem about the written Word. When the apostles took the Gospel to Gentiles, these peoples too came to love the written Word of God. That love for God's written Word has run like a bright thread through the history of the Christian church.

We are now engaged in a study of a part of God's written Word. In our LifeLight groups we are able to help and encourage one another in understanding and applying this Word. And, most wonderfully of all, the Holy Spirit is working through this Word to bring us to a more confident faith in our Savior, our Lord Jesus Christ, the Word made flesh!

Prayer

Read together the prayer from study leaflet 3.

Lecture Presentation

Introduction

In the previous lesson we learned how God's will, summarized in the Ten Commandments, was to be applied to the various dimensions of Israel's life. The Book of the Covenant ended with God's warning against making covenants with the inhabitants of Canaan and their gods, lest Israel abandon Yahweh for other gods. This week we are studying Exodus 24, which records the ratification of God's covenant with Israel. Before we look more closely at this chapter, however, it might be helpful to pause and remember what a covenant is and what

God's covenant with Israel was like. This will help us understand the new covenant we have in Christ.

Human covenants are treaties or agreements that two parties make with each other. God's covenant with Israel also was a relationship between two parties, God and Israel. However, in contrast to human pacts, which are *bilateral* (each party places obligations on the other), Yahweh's covenant with Israel was *unilateral*. Yahweh committed Himself to Israel and called Israel to be faithful to Him, but Israel could not place obligations on Yahweh. Also, unlike human covenants, Yahweh and Israel did not meet each other halfway. Rather, Yahweh took the initiative and delivered helpless Israel from Egyptian bondage and brought them to Himself (19:4).

At Sinai Yahweh entered into a covenant with Israel. The essence of this covenant is captured in the sentence we find frequently in the Old Testament, "I will . . . be your God and you will be My people" (Leviticus 26:12; Jeremiah 11:4; 30:22). Yahweh adopted the Israelites as His children, made them His people, and made Himself their God. Whenever the Israelites prayed to "the Lord our God," and whenever Moses said to them "the Lord your God," they were reminded of the covenant relationship and of their unique status as "a kingdom of priests and a holy nation," God's own possession (Exodus 19:5–6).

We have that same beautiful affirmation in the New Testament. Peter assured Gentile as well as Jewish believers (1 Peter 2:9–10): "But you are a chosen people, a royal priesthood, a holy nation, a people belonging to God, that you may declare the praises of Him who called you out of darkness into His wonderful light. Once you were not a people, but now you are the people of God; once you had not received mercy, but now you have received mercy."

We need to see this covenant God made with the Israelites through Moses as built on and flowing from the earlier covenant God had made with Abraham. This is indicated already back in Exodus 2:24, "God heard their groaning [in Egypt] and He remembered His covenant with Abraham, with Isaac, and with Jacob." When God reaffirmed His call to Moses, we find the same emphasis (Exodus 6:4–5): "I also established My covenant with them [that is, the patriarchs] to give them the land of Canaan, where they lived as aliens. Moreover, I have heard the groaning of the Israelites, whom the Egyptians are enslaving, and I have remembered My covenant."

God had promised to give Abraham numerous descendants, to bless him and his descendants, and to give them the land of Canaan. Because Yahweh faithfully remembered this covenant He made with Abraham, Isaac, and Jacob, He graciously brought their descendants out of Egyptian bondage to Himself. At Sinai God confirmed this grace-faith relationship with Israel. Exodus 24 records the ratification of this covenant.

This covenant God established with ancient Israel at Sinai prefigured and anticipated the new covenant that God in Christ has established with us. We too were helplessly in bondage to sin, death, and the devil. And the same God took the initiative and delivered us from this bondage, purely out of His grace and undeserved favor for the sake of Jesus Christ. Just as Israel did not come to God on its own power, neither did we. Instead, the Holy Spirit called us by the Gospel. God brought us to Himself, made us His own people, and made Himself our God in Christ. By means of Baptism He placed His name on us, so that now we belong to Him. And just as the old covenant was ratified by sacrifices and the blood of the covenant, so also the new covenant. By studying Exodus 24, we will learn what all is involved in the new covenant we have with our God.

1 Yahweh Calls His People to Him (24:1–2)

In these verses Yahweh calls the leaders to the mountain to worship and calls Moses alone to approach as covenant mediator.

In verse 1 God summons Moses, Aaron, Nadab, Abihu, and 70 of Israel's elders to ascend Mount Sinai and to worship God there. This event happens later in verses 9–11, when they ascend the mountain, see God, and eat and drink the covenant meal in fellowship with God. In verse 2 God summons Moses alone to approach God, so that God can give him further instructions. And this event occurs later in verses 12–18, when Moses enters the glory-cloud. But before they could approach God on the mountaintop, God's covenant with Israel at the bottom of the mountain first had to be solemnly ratified. That event is recorded in verses 3–8.

2 The Covenant Is Ratified (24:3–11)

The ceremony began with Moses proclaiming to the people the ten words of chapter 20 and the laws of chapters 21–23. All the people then respond with one voice (v. 3), "Everything the LORD has said we will do." This was a sincere response; they sincerely intended to lead a life worthy of their calling.

What brought about and called forth this Amen? It was the Word of God that Moses proclaimed. That divine Word is a powerful and active Word. It creates and sustains faith. Just as God's Word at creation, "Let there be," powerfully created, so His Word to ancient Israel and to us creates the response of Amen. God's powerful Word comes first; the people's response comes second. So it is when we worship. God's Word is central, not our words of response. His Word creates and sustains the church, and it produces our confession of faith. We are simply the sheep who hear the Shepherd's voice.

Notice how all the people responded in unison—"with one voice" (v. 3). Because God's Word is one, and because it creates the response, all of Israel responded as one people and with one voice. The church responds the same way. Each Christian does not invent his or her own confession of faith. Rather, we are taught the one true faith, and we all confess it in unison as we confess the church's creeds. Like ancient Israel, the church manifests her unity in the one faith by confessing that faith with the same words in unison.

The people responded, "Everything the LORD has said we will do." They did not receive God's words piecemeal, accepting this word but denying that one. God's Word comes as a whole, a unified package. They received it whole and said Amen to it all. Again, the same is true for us.

Verse 4 records that Moses wrote all the Lord's words and then prepared for the sacrifices by building an altar. He also set up 12 pillars as a memorial and sign to God and the people that all 12 tribes of Israel were included in this covenant.

At this time Moses had not yet ordained Levitical priests. Instead he simply designated some young men to offer the sacrifices on the newly built altar. They sacrificed young bulls as whole burnt offerings and fellowship offerings or peace offerings.

The whole burnt offering sacrificed and burned the whole animal, whereas the fellowship offering sacrificed the animal's fat portions, the two kidneys, and the appendage of the liver. These were considered the most valuable parts of the animal. The rest of the animal's meat was usually eaten by the worshiper and the priest in a communion meal before the Lord.

Leviticus 17:11 tells us that the Lord was the one who first set up the sacrificial system to make atonement for Israel. The idea is as follows. Sinners forfeit their right to life before the holy and just God. But instead of taking the life of the sinner, God in His grace takes the life of the animal as a substitute. Both the animal and its lifeblood go to the Lord in the place of the sinner, who deserves to die. The offering's smoke is a soothing odor for the Lord; the Lord turns away His own wrath by means of the sacrifice. God and the sinner are now one.

The entire system worked by virtue of the sacrifices' connection with Christ's perfect sacrifice, which they foreshadowed and prefigured. And the benefits of the atonement, the forgiveness of sins and life with God, were to be received by faith alone.

Moses again proclaimed the Word of God to the people by reading what he had written in verse 4. Again the powerful Word of God evoked the response (v. 7) "We will do everything the LORD has said; we will obey." Earlier, Moses had put the animals' blood into two basins and then splashed half of the blood against the altar. Thereby God received the animals' lifeblood in place of sinful Israel's lifeblood to make atonement. Now Moses splashed the other half of the same animals' blood on the people and said (v. 8), "This is the blood of the covenant that the LORD has made with you in accordance with all these words."

Except for seeing God on the mountaintop, this blood-rite at the bottom of the mountain was the highlight of the whole covenant ratification ceremony. By having the covenant blood splashed on them, the people were made the recipients and beneficiaries of the covenant God made with them. By this rite God confirmed Israel's status as God's forgiven people. Notice that the sentence says "the covenant that *the LORD* has made with you" (v. 8). Israel did not make the covenant relationship; God did, and Israel passively received it.

Moses drew their attention to the blood just splashed on them with the phrase (v. 8), "This is the blood of the covenant." God made and established them as His forgiven people with the blood of sacrifices. Moses wanted them to pay attention to the blood and to what God had done through the blood rather than to their own words of commitment.

What was so significant about the blood? It purified and cleansed them of their sins. Hebrews 9:20 quotes these words, and then in verse 22 it states: "In fact, the law requires that nearly everything be cleansed with blood, and without the shedding of blood there is no forgiveness." Leviticus 14 records the rite of cleansing for a person healed of an infectious skin disease. In this rite blood was sprinkled on the person, and the person was pronounced clean. In Exodus 29:19–21 the priests were consecrated to the Lord by having blood put on their right ear, the thumb of their right hand, the big toe of their right foot, and their garments.

In light of these parallels we can better understand the significance of this rite. By splashing the people with blood, God through Moses was cleansing them and consecrating them to Himself, as "a kingdom of priests and a holy nation" (Exodus 19:6).

In instituting the Lord's Supper, our Lord quoted from Exodus 24:8 as He said (Matthew 26:27–28): "Drink from it, all of you. This is My blood of the covenant, which is poured out for many for the forgiveness of sins." Just as ancient Israel received the blood of the covenant and thereby was cleansed, consecrated, and forgiven, so we as the new Israel receive the blood of the covenant in the Lord's Supper and thereby are cleansed, consecrated, and forgiven.

But notice the difference. Unlike ancient Israel, which was splashed with the blood only once, we drink the blood often. And Jesus added the pronoun *My*: "This is *My* blood of the covenant." The blood Moses splashed was the blood of sacrificial animals, but the blood we sacramentally drink in the Lord's Supper is the Lord's blood. The Lord shed His own blood on Calvary's cross and offered Himself as the perfect, all-sufficient sacrifice, which the animal sacrifices only prefigured. Thereby the Lord ratified the new covenant, made atonement, and obtained the forgiveness of our sins. In the Lord's Supper He gives us His blood to drink, and through it He delivers to us all the blessings of this new covenant, oneness with God as His own people and complete forgiveness. What a blessing we have in the Lord's Supper! Go to the Lord's Supper often and drink the Lord's blood of the new covenant!

After the solemn ceremony at the bottom of the mountain, Israel's representatives went to the top of the mountain. All of Israel could not go to the top. It would have been logistically impossible. But in effect all of Israel was there in and through their representatives.

And what a mountaintop experience it was! The text states in verse 10 that they "saw the God of Israel" and again in verse 11 that "they saw God, and they ate and drank." Of course, the text does not describe what God looked like. No Old Testament passage ever does. God does not want Israel to make an image that looked like Him. So it only describes the platform where God stood. It looked like (v. 10) "a pavement made of sapphire, clear as the sky itself." Heaven was on the top of that mountain!

But did they really see God? Yes indeed! God appeared to them in human form, since verse 10 mentions God's "feet." How does this square with 33:20, where God tells Moses, "No one may see Me and live"? No sinner may see God in all of His naked, overpowering, and brilliant majesty and continue to live. But the holy God on Mount Sinai clothed His majesty by appearing in human form and permitted Himself to be seen. Yes, they truly saw God and ate and drank the covenant meal in His presence.

The amazing thing is that (v. 11) "God did not raise His hand against these leaders of the Israelites." In chapter 19, when the Israelites first arrived at Mount Sinai, they were not permitted to even touch the mountain, let alone climb it. In 19:21 God instructs Moses, "Go down and warn the people so they do not force their way through to see the LORD and many of them perish." But now the Israelites, through their representatives, were permitted to see Yahweh.

What accounts for the difference? What happened was that the covenant was solemnly confirmed with the Word of God and the elicited Amen of the people and the sacrifices. What happened was that the blood of the covenant was splashed on the people. Because they had been cleansed, consecrated, and forgiven, they were now qualified to see God. The blood of the covenant made the difference.

So also with us. Because we have been called by the

Gospel, because we have been made God's covenant people through Baptism, because we drink the Lord's blood of the new covenant, which the Lord sacrificed on the cross for us, we have the assurance and promise that we too will see the Lord at His Second Coming. As 1 John 3:2 promises us, "When He appears, we shall be like Him, for we shall see Him as He is."

The Lord's Supper gives us a foretaste and guarantee of the future heavenly banquet we will enjoy with the Lord (Revelation 19:7–9). Then we will see God and eat and drink as did Israel's representatives. In fact, the Lord's Supper gives us even more. In Exodus 24 the two events were separate in time. The Israelites received the blood of the covenant at the bottom of the mountain, and they saw God, ate, and drank at the top of the mountain. In the Lord's Supper these two events are brought together; the bottom and the top of the mountain events are united. Now we eat the Lord's body and drink His blood of the covenant at the same time. Even now we are privileged to see the Lord, though in hidden form behind the bread and wine. What blessings the Lord gives us in His Supper! What could be more wonderful than to share in communion at His table with the same God who appeared to ancient Israel?

3 Moses Spends Time with God (24:12–18)

After this mountaintop experience Moses alone went up farther on the mountain to receive additional revelation from God. The additional revelation concerned the tabernacle and priesthood, which would serve as the means by which Yahweh continued to commune with Israel. Moses now entered the glory-cloud (which we will study in lesson 9) and stayed on the mountain 40 days and nights.

Closing Activities

Close the session with a prayer thanking God for the opportunities He gives us to study His Word together, to be received into His new covenant through Holy Baptism, and to have that covenant ratified each time we receive the Lord's Supper. Then make any necessary announcements, share any questions or comments about the enrichment magazine, and distribute study leaflet 4.

The Tabernacle and Its Furnishings

Exodus 25–27

Preparing for the Session

Central Focus

This session discusses the tabernacle and its furnishings. The lesson will focus particularly on the significance of the furniture.

Objectives

That the participant will be led to

1. repent of sin against God;
2. believe in the forgiveness achieved by the atoning sacrifice of Jesus Christ;
3. frequently go to the means of grace to receive this forgiveness from the Lord;
4. rejoice in the tabernacling presence of God in Christ among His people;
5. appreciate more fully that the Lord delivered the church in order to dwell in her midst and evoke her worship.

Note for the small-group leaders: Lesson notes and other materials you will need begin on page 63.

Session Plan

Worship

Begin the session with the hymn and prayer printed in the study leaflet. (Accompaniments are available in denominational hymnals, such as *Lutheran Worship* [refer to hymnal index], or on the *Every Voice a Song* CD set.) Continue with this devotion:

Devotion

Our daily personal devotions, and even our worship in larger groups, may take the simplest of forms and routines. After all, as Jesus said, the requirements of worship are only that we "worship in spirit and in truth" (John 4:24). But our Bible study this week provides the biblical background for the supporting accessories of worship commonly used in our churches.

We would do well to plan the moments of our personal devotions, even though they may be simple in form, with care and reverence, just as God carefully planned the worship of the Israelites. We may pick a particularly pleasant spot for our daily devotions, at a time and place most conducive to devotional concentration. God instructed the Israelites, even when a nomadic people, to recognize and appreciate His presence and to worship Him with reverence, even in the harsh surroundings of the Sinai wilderness.

We surely don't want to play at our devotions and Bible study or to engage in them either halfheartedly or habitually. God deserves our best efforts and fullest attention. The place we select to approach Him in awe and reverence may be plain and simple, but in our worship we have built our tabernacle and have furnished our lives with the essentials that elevate the common to the sacred.

Lecture Presentation

Introduction

In Exodus 20–24 we have seen how the Lord covenanted with His people. The rest of Exodus in chapters 25–31 and 35–40 focuses on how the Lord tabernacles with His people. In Exodus the tabernacle was the portable tent or shrine in which God dwelt. It was Israel's sanctuary for several centuries, from the time it was set up at Sinai until Solomon built the temple in Jerusalem about 960 B.C. The verb *to tabernacle* means "to dwell," so that the phrase means "the Lord dwells in the tabernacle with His people."

We have seen how the Lord made Israel His own people and how He sealed this covenant grace-faith relationship by means of the Word, sacrifices, and the blood of the covenant. Yet this was not the end of His dealings with His people. How would the Lord maintain this covenant relationship and continue to abide with the

Israelites after they left Sinai? The answer came in the form of the tabernacle. The Lord delivered the Israelites from Egypt in order to tabernacle among them and be their God (29:45–46).

These chapters of Scripture are not as well known as those that tell us about the 10 plagues and the exodus, but they are no less important. The whole tabernacle complex held rich meaning and significance for the ancient Israelites. It still holds rich theological meaning for us.

First, the texts referring to the tabernacle reveal what is necessary for the holy God to dwell among sinners and for sinners to stand before the holy God. The tabernacle complex is a large-scale visual aid that shows the necessity of atonement. It was also a means of grace in the Old Testament. By means of the sacrifices and sacrificial blood, it portrayed the coming Holy One, who would be the perfect sacrifice for sin.

Second, these texts about the tabernacle will help us appreciate more fully who we are as God's worshiping people. The tabernacle, where God graciously dwelt in Israel's midst and blessed them, was to be the center of Israel's life.

So also with us. Through Baptism we have been tied to the Lord and incorporated into the Lord's church (1 Corinthians 12:13). The Lord's church is the assembly of believers among whom the Lord graciously tabernacles, forgives sins, and gives life through the Gospel and Sacraments administered by the pastor. Those gifts then cause us to respond in praise and prayer. At the center of our life together as the new Israel is our worship. We have been saved in order to worship.

1 The Tabernacle (25:1–9)

In chapters 25–31, while Moses is on the mountain 40 days and nights, Yahweh instructs him how Israel is to build the tabernacle and its furnishings. The Lord begins by asking the Israelites to contribute voluntarily the necessary materials. The Lord's gracious covenant motivated and inspired the Israelites to give of their time, talents, and treasures with gratitude. (2 Corinthians 9:7) "God loves a cheerful giver."

Verses 8–9 are extremely important for understanding the meaning and significance of the tabernacle. It is called a sanctuary, a holy place, because the holy God will dwell there, and it is called a tabernacle, a dwelling, because the holy God will dwell there.

The almighty Creator of the universe cannot, of course, be confined in a tent or building made by human creatures. As Solomon acknowledged when he dedicated the temple in Jerusalem (1 Kings 8:27): "But will God really dwell on earth? The heavens, even the highest heaven, cannot contain You. How much less this temple I have built!"

In light of the Lord's exaltedness, it is truly amazing that He instructed Israel to build a dwelling for Him and promised to dwell in Israel's midst. God made His gracious presence and gifts accessible to the space- and time-bound Israelites. He located Himself in space and time. Israel would not journey to Canaan alone; their God would go with them.

The same is true for us. The tabernacle in which God dwelt with His people pointed ahead to God's becoming man in Jesus. As John 1:14 says, "The Word [God Himself] became flesh and made His dwelling among us." The verb *dwelt* literally means "tabernacled." Jesus Christ is the new and greater tabernacle (Colossians 1:19; 2:9): "For God was pleased to have all His fullness dwell in Him." And where do we, the new Israel, find the exalted Lord Jesus Christ? We find Him where He promises to be for us, in the Gospel, in Baptism, and in the Lord's Supper. Go to those places and find His gracious presence and gifts for you. And rejoice that the exalted and holy Lord promises to go with you on your journey to the Promised Land.

In verse 9 God instructs Moses to make the tabernacle and its furnishings "exactly like the pattern" God shows him. Hebrews 8:2, 5 tells us that Israel's tabernacle was an earthly copy and shadow of the original heavenly tabernacle that God Himself set up. Israel's tabernacle was an earthly miniature of the perfect heavenly tabernacle and dwelling of God; it was heaven on earth.

2 The Furniture (25:10–22)

This section gives instructions concerning the construction of the furniture that would be located in the Most Holy Place (or Holy of Holies): the ark, its atonement cover, and the two cherubim. The ark was simply a chest or box made of wood and overlaid with gold. Inside the ark were placed the "Testimony," that is, the two stone tablets containing the Ten Commandments, a pot of manna (Exodus 16:33–34), and Aaron's rod that budded to indicate that the Lord had chosen Aaron and his descendants to serve as high priest (Numbers 17:10–11).

The two stone tablets gave testimony to the covenant; the pot of manna commemorated God's gracious care for Israel in the wilderness; and Aaron's rod witnessed to God's choice of the tribe of Levi as the priestly line. These items contained in the ark served to remind not only Israel but also God of His promises and care for Israel. We, too, have been given the privilege of reminding God of His gracious promises in Christ. When the Gospel is preached and the Sacraments are administered, certainly we are reminded of His promises, but also He is reminded. We can truly be confident that He will faithfully keep His promises to us.

Over the ark lay an "atonement cover" or "mercy seat" of pure gold. On this atonement cover the high priest made atonement for Israel's sins by sprinkling on it the sacrificial blood. This happened once a year on the Day of Atonement (Leviticus 16). In order for the holy God to continue dwelling among the sinful Israelites, both the people and His dwelling place needed to be cleansed. What a powerful picture and anticipation of Jesus Christ's cleansing blood this is! (1 John 1:7) "The blood of Jesus, His Son, cleanses us from all sin." It cleanses the church, which is (2 Corinthians 6:16) "the temple of the living God."

Moses was also instructed to make two symbolic figures called cherubim out of gold (*cherubim* is the plural of *cherub*), one cherub for the north end of the ark and one cherub for the south end of the ark. A cherub resembled a hybrid animal—a lion's body with a human head and eagles' wings. In the ancient world cherubim represented a king's throne. Also, the ark and cherubim in the Most Holy Place were seen as the throne or footstool of a king (1 Chronicles 28:2; Psalm 99:1, 5; 132:7). But this King was no ordinary king; He was and is the King of kings and Lord of lords. There in the Most Holy Place Yahweh the King sat enthroned, and from there He ruled Israel and the world.

The New Testament often states that Christ is the exalted King who rules His church, the new Israel, and the world. He sits enthroned at the very right hand of the Father in heaven. From there He rules all things to the benefit of His church. We can see best what kind of King He is from the cross. As He hung on the cross and died for the sins of the whole world, the inscription above His head read, "This is Jesus the King of the Jews" (Matthew 27:37). He was no more "kingly" than at that moment. What a marvelous King we have, one who gave Himself for His enemies! And now as the resurrected and ascended Lord He continues to rule graciously through the Gospel and Sacraments.

3 The Table and Lampstand (25:23–40)

This section deals with two of the three pieces of furniture in the Holy Place, namely the table for the bread of the Presence (showbread) and the lampstand. The table was made of acacia wood and overlaid with pure gold. On it were laid four golden utensils: dishes for the bread, flagons that held wine for the drink offering, bowls that held oil for the lampstand, and spoons for incense. Also, 12 cakes of bread set in two rows of six were placed on the table (Leviticus 24:5–9). This is called "the bread of the Presence" or "the showbread," because it was to be set before God's "presence" at all times. Every Sabbath the priests replaced the old bread with freshly baked bread. The priests then had the old bread to eat. Thus, the offerings the people made to the Lord became provisions for the priests (Leviticus 24:9), just as our offerings are used to support the minister (1 Corinthians 9:13–14).

The lampstand, made out of one piece of gold, consisted of a central shaft and three arms or branches protruding outward and upward on two sides of the shaft. Upon each of the seven stems rested an oval dish containing oil for burning. The lamps were to burn perpetually before Yahweh from evening till morning (27:20–21). Obviously, the lampstand provided light for the otherwise dark Holy Place (25:37). Although the text does not inform us of any further meaning, we can infer from the rest of the Old Testament that the lampstand witnessed to Yahweh as the perpetual "light" to Israel and through Israel to the nations.

4 The Tent (26)

Chapter 26 describes the tent itself. It had four fabric coverings over its top, which served as its roof. Five square pillars stood at the door of the tent, which separated the tent from the courtyard. Four pillars stood in the tent to mark the dividing point between the Holy Place and the Most Holy Place. These pillars were made of acacia wood overlaid with gold, and they measured 15 feet high. Hanging from the four pillars was the veil or curtain. It was made of blue, purple, and scarlet dyed wool plus white linen and also had cherubim woven in.

The pillars and veil testified to the separation between the holy God and sinful Israel. Only priests were allowed to enter the Holy Place. Only the high priest once a year, on the Day of Atonement, could enter the Most Holy Place. One must be holy and whole to stand before the holy God. Christ is the new and greater High Priest, who has entered heaven itself with His perfect atonement (Hebrews 9:24). In Him we have all been made holy and whole priests and can now with confidence (Hebrews 10:19–20) "enter the Most Holy Place by the blood of Jesus, by a new and living way opened for us through the curtain, that is, His body." He has paved the way and given us all a direct access to God Himself.

5 The Altar of Sacrifice (27)

Chapter 27 deals with the sacrificial altar, the courtyard, and the oil for the lampstand. We will discuss the courtyard in lesson 9. Here we will focus on the altar. The altar in the courtyard was to be made of acacia wood overlaid with bronze. Its dimensions were three cubits high, five cubits long, and five cubits wide. Normally a cubit covered the length from one's elbow to the tip of the middle finger. In ancient times there existed a royal cubit of about 20.6 inches and an ordinary cubit of about 18 inches. On the basis of the latter, the altar was 4.5 feet high and 7.5 feet long and wide. It had four hornlike projections at the four top corners.

This altar was, of course, where sacrifices were to be offered by the priests. Israel had five types of sacrifices, which are described in Leviticus 1–7: the whole burnt offering, the grain (or cereal) offering, the fellowship (or peace) offering, the sin offering, and the guilt offering. Each one had its own unique significance and is worthy of further study.

Basically these various types of sacrifices had four purposes: to make atonement for sins so that the sinner could be forgiven; to purify and cleanse with sacrificial blood the altar and tabernacle from the pollution caused by Israel's sins and impurities; to enable the worshiper to share in a communion meal with the priest before God; and to offer a token of one's entire self as a sacrifice of dedication and thanks in response to God's undeserved grace.

In all four respects Jesus Christ sums up and fulfills the meaning of these sacrifices by offering Himself as the perfect and all-sufficient sacrifice on the altar of the cross. Christ has made atonement for the sins of the whole world. His blood cleanses the church from the "cosmic" impurity caused by the world's polluting sins. In Him we have fellowship and communion with God. His sacrifice of complete dedication covers our unfaithfulness and lack of gratitude. Because of His work we are empowered by the Spirit to offer ourselves as living sacrifices, holy and pleasing to God.

Closing Activities

Speak a brief prayer (perhaps thanking Jesus for His sacrifice to make atonement for our sin). Then distribute study leaflet 5.

The Priesthood

Exodus 28–29

Preparing for the Session

Central Focus

This session discusses the Old Testament priesthood—its garments, ordination, and roles—and shows how it relates to Christ, the ministers of the Gospel, and the priesthood of all believers.

Objectives

That the participant will be led to

1. repent of sins, which make it impossible to stand before the holy God without a mediator;
2. believe in the Lord Jesus Christ, who is the High Priest and atoning sacrifice for all;
3. receive by faith the forgiveness and holiness that Christ bestows through the ministers of the Gospel;
4. appreciate more fully his or her role as a priest of God in Christ;
5. eagerly await the Last Day, when believers will be made perfect and whole and will enter the heavenly sanctuary to be with the Lord forever.

Note for the small-group leaders: Lesson notes and other materials you will need begin on page 6.

Session Plan

For the Lecture Leader

Again, visual aids might be helpful for picturing the garments of the high priest. One can find color pictures in either Paul F. Kiene's *The Tabernacle of God in the Wilderness of Sinai* (Grand Rapids, MI: Zondervan, 1977) or Paul M. Zehr's *God Dwells with His People* (Scottsdale, PA: Herald Press, 1981).

Session Plan

Worship

Begin the session with the hymn and prayer printed in the study leaflet. (Accompaniments are available in denominational hymnals, such as *Lutheran Worship* [refer to hymnal index], or on the *Every Voice a Song* CD set.) Continue with this devotion:

Devotion

This week's Scripture reading and study will focus on the priesthood of the people of Israel. We will see parallels between that priesthood and our pastoral ministry today. But there is also a great difference. Old Testament priests offered sacrifices to God on the altar in the tabernacle courtyard on behalf of the Israelites. Only the priests could approach God in the Holy Place of the tabernacle to acknowledge God's gifts to His people and to commit the people to God in thankful service with the offering of the 12 loaves of bread on the table, one loaf for each tribe. And only the high priest could enter the Most Holy Place, where God's presence was symbolized in the ark containing the Ten Commandments and His throne envisioned in the ark's "mercy seat," with its two facing cherubim.

The difference between the Israelites' situation and our own is this: Jesus Christ took the place of the high priest and offered Himself for us, once and for all. In this way He opened the way for us into the presence of God, so that we too—formerly hostage to our sins and the power of the devil but now set free by Christ—can enter the Most Holy Place. Because of Him, we become a holy priesthood too, committed to God.

Christ gives to our worship, individually and collectively, the authority to draw near to God, through Christ as our intermediary, without the priestly or ministerial office. We accept the ministry as instituted by Christ, but we see it not in place of Christ but in service to Him for our sakes, so that "everything should be done in a fitting and orderly way" (1 Corinthians 14:40). We need no earthly priest to represent us before

God or to give us access to Him, for we have "a High Priest, who sat down at the right hand of the throne of the Majesty in heaven, and who serves in the sanctuary, the true tabernacle set up by the Lord, not by man" (Hebrews 8:1–2).

Lecture Presentation

Introduction

In the last lesson we began to see how the Lord tabernacles with His people. For that to occur, Israel was to build a tabernacle and its various articles of furniture. But a tabernacle needs officiants to attend to it and offer the sacrifices. In this lesson we will first discuss the garments and role of the priests. We will find that this all has tremendous significance for us today in relation to the person and work of Christ, to the church's ministers, and to all of us as priests of God.

1 God's Nearness and Priestly Mediation

For the holy God to dwell among sinners, a mediation had to take place, and that mediation came in the form of the tabernacle complex and the priests. We have this paradox of God's nearness on the one hand and of the need for priestly mediation on the other hand.

Both of these elements come together in Jesus Christ. In Him God is very near. In fact, Jesus is Immanuel, "God with us," the incarnate God Himself, who dwells among us through Word and Sacrament. And He is the mediator who reconciles the holy God with us sinners (1 Timothy 2:5), "For there is one God and one mediator between God and men, the man Christ Jesus."

2 The Priestly Garments

Although Aaron sinned against God in the golden-calf apostasy (Exodus 32), he was still ordained in Leviticus 8. From then on Aaron's line of the tribe of Levi would become the priestly line. The other Levites were to serve as ministerial assistants.

The priests were to be invested with special garments (28:2–5). The ordinary priests wore linen undergarments, tunics, sashes, and headbands (28:40–43). The high priest Aaron wore linen undergarments, a tunic, a robe, an ephod, a breastpiece, a sash, and a turban. The undergarments were made of white linen and worn for the purpose of modesty and decency (20:26). The tunic of white linen covered the entire body and extended to the ground. Over the tunic lay a blue robe. It covered the entire body except the arms and extended down to 6 inches above the ground. At its bottom were fabric pomegranates and golden bells. As the high priest walked inside the sanctuary the bells rang, thereby indicating to the assembled Israelites that he was alive and well when he carried out his duties in the tabernacle. They also served to prevent his death (28:35).

Over the blue robe lay the ephod (28:6–14), an apron-like garment with straps over each shoulder. It was woven with gold, blue, purple, and scarlet yarn and finely twisted linen. Upon the straps over the shoulders lay two onyx stones, one on each shoulder. Each stone had six names of the tribes of Israel engraved in the order of their birth. A sash or belt, about 6 inches wide and woven like the ephod, went around the middle of the high priest and was tied in front to keep the ephod tight to his body.

A fabric breastplate (28:15–30), 18 inches long and 9 inches wide and woven similar to the ephod, covered the chest. In the middle it was folded to form a square pocket in which were placed the Urim and Thummim. Twelve different precious stones engraved with the names of the 12 tribes rested on the breastplate. A turban of fine linen served as the headgear. Across the front a gold plate was fastened, on which were written the words "Holy to Yahweh."

These vestments were rich in meaning and significance. They indicated that the priests, and especially the high priest, were distinguished by God from the rest of the Israelites in order to function as mediators between the holy God and sinful Israel. But how could the priests and high priest do this, given their own sinfulness? The holy God conferred His holiness on them by means of investing them with these special garments. (See Psalm 132:9.) They are called "sacred garments" (28:2). They were made "to consecrate" or set apart Aaron for God's priesthood (28:3). Without the garments the priests would die when they approached the holy God in the tabernacle and the altar (28:35, 43).

Aaron's garments were intended "for glory and for beauty" (28:2 RSV). The word translated "for glory" in the RSV is the same word mentioned in 24:16, "and the glory of the LORD settled on Mount Sinai" and in 40:34, "and the glory of the LORD filled the tabernacle." The "glory of the LORD" on the top of Sinai looked like a fiery cloud and that same "glory of the LORD" filled the tabernacle. In the fiery cloud the glorious Lord was present. Aaron's garments and the priests' garments (28:40) reflected this glory. The dazzling splendor and beauty of the garments reflected and revealed the dazzling splendor and beauty of the holy God. This beauty of God was revealed by the beauty of the garments. How the ancient Israelites must have eagerly awaited the day when they, and we too, will see the Lord face-to-face in all of His splendid beauty.

Notice that the high priest's garments matched the materials of the inner parts of the tabernacle. The garments, as the curtains, were made of fine linen, using gold, blue, purple, and scarlet (26:1–6; 28:5–8). The high priest was brought into the sphere of the holy God, and therefore his garments matched the tabernacle's material. He was, as it were, a co-dweller with God in that domain.

Three features of the high priest's garments carried special significance. First, the Urim and Thummim (28–30), which were apparently lots carried inside the pouch of the breastpiece, were used to determine the will of God in a given situation.

Second, the high priest bore the names of the 12 tribes both on his two shoulder stones and on his breastpiece. Thereby he represented Israel before God and reminded God of His commitment and covenant promises toward all of Israel (28:12, 29).

Third, the gold plate on Aaron's turban, which read "Holy to Yahweh," conferred and imputed Yahweh's holiness to sinful Aaron. Because Aaron was thus "holied" and hallowed, he would "bear the guilt involved in the sacred gifts the Israelites consecrate" (28:38). The turban was on Aaron's head continually, so that the Israelites' offerings would be "acceptable to the LORD" (28:38). But Aaron was hallowed, so that as a substitute he could bear Israel's guilt and yet not be punished.

3 The Priestly Roles

The priests functioned as mediators between the holy God and sinful Israel. The priests were double representatives: God's representatives to Israel and Israel's representatives to God.

The priests' role as God's representatives to Israel can be seen in the following ways:

A. By means of the sacrifices and the sacrificial blood, the priests made atonement for the Israelites' sins. On this basis they absolved the sinner of sins (Leviticus 5:10, 13, 16, 18; 6:7).

B. The priests blessed the Israelites and put the Lord's name on them by pronouncing the Aaronic benediction (Numbers 6:22–27).

C. The priests and Levites were ministers of the Word of God. They preserved the Word of God (Deuteronomy 31:9) and taught it to the people (Leviticus 10:11; Deuteronomy 31:9; Malachi 2:7). They also settled disputes with the Urim and Thummim and the Word of God (Exodus 28:30; Deuteronomy 17:8–13; 19:17; 21:5).

D. By wearing the priestly garments that were "for glory and beauty," the priests revealed to Israel the glory and beauty of the Lord (28:2, 40).

While Israel was designated a "kingdom of priests" in 19:6, not all were required to serve as priests. In the people's place and on their behalf the Aaronic priesthood represented Israel to God in the following ways:

A. Aaron embodied all of Israel before Yahweh; he was Israel—reduced to one. In and through Aaron, all Israel was "Holy to Yahweh" as inscribed on his turban (28:36; translated in NIV as "HOLY TO THE LORD").

B. As Israel's substitute, Aaron bore Israel's guilt, so that Israel's tainted offerings were acceptable to the Lord (28:38).

C. Aaron bore the names of the 12 tribes on his shoulder stones and his breastpiece. In this way when he came before the Lord, he brought all of Israel before the Lord. This reminded the Lord of His commitment and covenant promises to the people (28:12, 29).

D. The priests and Levites led the assembled congregation in prayer and praise to God (Psalms; 1 Chronicles 23–25).

4 Christ the High Priest

While God bestowed the gifts of His grace through the ministry of the Old Testament priests, that ministry was valid and effective only by virtue of the work of Christ. That priestly ministry was not the perfect and all-sufficient priestly ministry, but it served as a pointer to Christ, who is the perfect and all-sufficient Priest. Thus, the Aaronic priesthood prefigured and anticipated the new and greater High Priest, Jesus Christ.

A. Both the priests and Christ were appointed by God, but Christ's high priesthood came directly from God apart from Moses and the old legislation.

B. The priests' garments reflected God's glory and holiness, but Christ manifests God's glory and holiness in Himself.

C. The priests at different times entered a tabernacle made by human hands to intercede, but Christ entered the heavenly sanctuary and forever intercedes.

D. The priests offered sacrifices many times for Israel and themselves, but the sinless Christ offered Himself as the all-sufficient and once-for-all sacrifice, which atones for the sins of the whole world.

E. The priests sprinkled with animal blood, but Christ purifies our conscience with His own blood.

F. The priesthood passed on from father to son, but Christ's office continues at the right hand of the Father.

G. The priests were mediators between God and Israel, but Christ is both mediator and God.

5 Pastor as Priest

The Old Testament priests were to be males who served as ministers of the Word of God. They taught the Word and blessed the people by pronouncing the Aaronic benediction. They administered the means by which the people received the forgiveness of sins. They also led the people in prayer and praise to God. In these respects today's pastors stand in continuity with the ancient priests. St. Paul sees a continuity between Old Testament priests and New Testament ministers of the Gospel (Romans 15:16; 1 Corinthians 9:13–14).

Obviously, there are differences. The pastor does not mediate through a holier status or through offering atoning sacrifices. Through Christ's all-sufficient atoning sacrifice, all believers are equally holy. Nor is the pastoral ministry limited to the tribe of Levi. Nevertheless, the center of the pastoral ministry is still blood and sacrifice—that of Christ. By preaching the atoning sacrifice of Christ, by pronouncing absolution and God's blessing, and by administering the Sacraments, the pastor—as a called and ordained servant of the Word, in the stead and by the command of Christ our High Priest—is involved in a "priestly" ministry.

6 All Believers as Priests

Because of Christ's high priestly work, all Christians have been elevated to the status of priests (1 Peter 2:9). All believers are clothed with the beautiful garments of Christ's holiness and righteousness. There are no longer degrees of holiness; in Christ we have all been equally "holied" by faith. As priests in Christ we all serve God (Revelation 1:6), offer ourselves as living sacrifices, holy and acceptable to God (Romans 12:1), and declare the wonderful deeds of Him who called us out of darkness into His marvelous light (1 Peter 2:9).

By studying the nature and functions of the Old Testament priesthood, we grow in our understanding of Christ's person and work, of the priestly ministry of our pastors, and of our high and holy status as priests ourselves. It leads us to sing a doxology with the words of Revelation 1:5–6: "To Him who loves us and has freed us from our sins by His blood, and has made us to be a kingdom and priests to serve His God and Father—to Him be glory and power for ever and ever! Amen."

7 The Consecration and Ordination of Priests

In chapter 29 God instructs Moses how to consecrate and ordain Aaron and his sons into the priesthood and how to consecrate the altar. In the original language the word *consecrate* comes from the same root as the word *holy.* "To holy" or "to consecrate" someone means to set one apart from the rest and to God. Just as Israel was set apart from other nations to be God's "holy nation," so Aaron and his sons were to be set apart from the rest of the Israelites and made God's priests.

The rites of priestly consecration and ordination included the following steps: washing with water, investing with "holy" garments, anointing with oil, offering animal sacrifices, and sprinkling with blood. Finally came the sacred meal, during which Aaron and his sons ate the ram's meat and bread. The whole ceremony was to be repeated for seven days.

What happened by means of this seven-day ceremony? Aaron and his sons were installed into the priestly office and consecrated to God's service. Aaron as high priest had his head anointed with oil. Just as kings Saul (1 Samuel 10:1, 6) and David (1 Samuel 16:13–14) were later anointed with oil and the Holy Spirit, so also the high priest. Aaron and his sons placed their own sins on the animals, and the animals were sacrificed in their place to make atonement for them. Finally, in a sacred meal they ate of what made atonement.

All of this is summed up and fulfilled by Christ. He, too, was anointed with the Spirit at His Baptism. He, too, as the great High Priest offered Himself as the perfect sacrifice to atone not for His own sins but for the sins of the whole world, your sins and mine. And He has made us all priests; we have been invested with the garments of His righteousness and holiness. We as priests have been anointed with the Holy Spirit through Baptism. We as priests have been sprinkled and cleansed with His blood. And we as priests have the wonderful opportunity of sharing in the sacred meal of the Lord's Supper, a far more glorious meal than that of the priests' meal. In Christ God continues to tabernacle among His people, and by faith we truly know Him as our God (vv. 45–46). What rich treasures this part of Scripture reveals to us, the new Israel!

Concluding Activities

Offer a brief prayer suggested by this lesson, make any necessary announcements, and distribute study leaflet 6.

The Elements of Worship

Exodus 30–31

Preparing for the Session

Central Focus

This session deals with the tabernacle's incense altar and bronze basin and with the ransom money, the workers' God-given skill, and the Sabbath. It will concentrate on the tabernacle's significance for the church's liturgical worship.

Objectives

That the participant will be led to

1. repent of sins against God;
2. believe in the forgiveness of sins that comes from Christ, who paid the ransom price in his or her place;
3. rejoice in the washing of regeneration received in Baptism;
4. attend church to receive the means of grace;
5. appreciate more fully the church's historic liturgy;
6. thank God for the skills and abilities He has given so he or she might serve Him.

Note for the small-group leaders: Lesson notes and other materials you will need begin on page 69.

Session Plan

Worship

Begin the session with the hymn printed in the study leaflet. (Accompaniments are available in denominational hymnals, such as *Lutheran Worship* [refer to hymnal index], or on the *Every Voice a Song* CD set.) Then conclude the group worship by reading together the prayer from the study leaflet.

Lecture Presentation

Introduction

The Israelites were delivered from Egypt in order to be the Lord's worshiping community gathered around the means of grace. In this lesson we will discuss further how the tabernacle and the worship connected with it can help us understand and appreciate more fully the church's worship practices.

1 The Incense Altar (30:1–10)

Moses was instructed to make an altar for burning incense. It was to be located at the west end of the Holy Place in front of the curtain separating the Holy Place from the Most Holy Place. This altar, made of acacia wood overlaid with gold and having four corner horns, measured 1½ feet square and 3 feet high.

Only incense was to be offered at the incense altar. In offering incense Aaron would take burning coals from the sacrificial altar, place them on the incense altar, and spread over them the incense powder of spices. The incense burned every morning and evening so that it burned regularly before Yahweh.

Why was incense important? Old Testament passages indicate that it provided a sweet-smelling aroma that pleased God. For the holy God to dwell among sinners was always dangerous for the sinners because of God's just wrath against sin. But God provided a means that would turn away His wrath, and that was the incense aroma (Leviticus 2:1; Numbers 16:46–50). On the Day of Atonement the incense created a screen that prevented the sinful high priest from gazing on the holy God and dying.

It also symbolized the believer's prayers, in which God delighted (Psalm 141:2): "May my prayer be set before You like incense; may the lifting up of my hands be like the evening sacrifice." In the New Testament incense also provides a picture of the saints' prayers coming before God as a sweet-smelling aroma (Revelation 5:8; 8:3).

Have you ever been in a worship service in which there was incense? Perhaps the smell seemed strange to you. But the use of incense is really quite a beautiful symbol. It reminds us of Christ's perfect sacrifice offered once and for all on the cross and of how that sacrifice turned away God's just wrath and pleases Him. It reminds us of how our prayers in Christ's name are lifted up before God and delight Him as a sweet-smelling aroma.

And perhaps the strangeness of the smell is a good thing. During the week from Monday to Saturday we experience the everyday sights and sounds and smells of life. But on Sunday morning, when we come before God in church, we enter a different realm, a heavenly realm where the sights and smells and sounds are different, a realm where the holy God is present in His Word and Sacraments. During that hour even our smells are like the smells of heaven (Revelation 5:8; 8:3). The incense used in the tabernacle was also to be unique and unlike the incense used normally by the Israelites (30:34–38).

Verse 10 mentions that once a year Aaron had to make atonement with sacrificial blood on the incense altar's horns. This rite was part of the ceremony done on the annual day of atonement described in Leviticus 16. There we learn that Aaron was to sprinkle blood with his finger seven times on the incense altar "to cleanse it and to consecrate it from the uncleanness of the Israelites" (Leviticus 16:19).

The sacrificial blood would act as a kind of detergent to purify God's dwelling from the sins of the people.

If (Hebrews 9:22) "the law requires that nearly everything be cleansed with blood, and without the shedding of blood there is no forgiveness," how much more does Christ's blood purify His temple, the church, and even heaven itself!

2 The Atonement Money (30:11–16)

In these verses God instructs Moses concerning the census of the Israelites he was to take (see Numbers 1). When each Israelite male from 20 years old and up came to the tabernacle to be numbered, he was to pay ransom money to Yahweh for his life. Everyone, whether rich or poor, was to give the same amount as an offering. The amount was half a shekel. That atonement money was then to be used for the service of the tabernacle.

This helps us to learn more of what is needed for sinners to stand before the holy God. If a sinner approached the holy God's holy dwelling place without a ransom, he would die. The holy God would then send a plague (v. 12). Also, a sinner could not on his own initiative and on the basis of his own merits stand before God. A ransom was needed. Here God Himself set up the ransom method. The same idea is in 21:28–32, where the negligent owner of a bull that killed someone could redeem his life by paying a ransom price. It was deliverance from death by a ransom payment.

Perhaps when we think of ransom money, we think of paying off kidnappers or terrorists. But such an idea would be misleading in this case because God is holy. Perhaps a better analogy comes from the world of sports. If a highly paid athlete does not play well for several months, fans begin to say that the athlete should be removed from the team. But then, if the athlete plays well and wins the game, the fans say that the athlete redeemed himself or herself.

Similarly, each Israelite man was in danger of being removed from the people of God unless he redeemed himself with a ransom. But here God initiated and set up the ransom method. The money was used for the tabernacle's bases and pillars (38:25–28). In this way it would (30:16) "be a memorial for the Israelites before the LORD, making atonement for your lives."

What a powerful picture of the work of Christ this offers us! Each one of us is by nature a lost and condemned creature, under the wrath of God and in danger of eternal death. But God sent His one and only Son to redeem us and purchase us (1 Peter 1:18–19) "not with perishable things such as silver or gold . . . but with the precious blood of Christ, a lamb without blemish or defect." And to what end? (2 Corinthians 5:15) "That those who live should no longer live for themselves but for Him who died for them and was raised again."

Deliverance from death and life with the holy God comes only at a price. God's grace is not cheap. It is costly, very costly. But unlike the Israelites' payment of the ransom price, we do not ransom ourselves with money. Instead, God Himself paid the price, a price more costly than money. At the cost of the death of His own Son God redeemed us. (Mark 10:45) "The Son of Man did not come to be served, but to serve, and to give His life as a ransom for many." And that "many" includes you! (1 Corinthians 6:19–20) "You are not your own; you were bought at a price. Therefore honor God with your body." And the ransom price that Christ paid has eternal consequences. It is an "eternal redemption" that continues to remind God that we are His redeemed people (Hebrews 9:12).

3 The Basin for Washing (30:17–21)

Now God instructs Moses to make a bronze basin and to place it between the tent and the sacrificial altar in the courtyard. The basin was made from the mirrors contributed by the women (38:8). All of the Israelites contributed to the tabernacle. This basin or laver was filled with water for the purpose of the priestly washings. When the priests were consecrated to the priesthood, their entire body was washed at the basin (Exodus 29:4; Leviticus 8:6). Also, whenever the priests entered the tent or ministered at the sacrificial altar, they washed their hands and feet. The stated purpose is "so that they will not die" (30:21). Again we see how important being cleansed and purified were. Much more than simple hygiene was involved. Without washing they were unfit to serve before the Lord and would die. To be holy as a priest involved physical as well as spiritual purity and cleanliness.

This points to Baptism. Baptism is (Titus 3:5) "the washing of rebirth and renewal by the Holy Spirit." Christ cleansed the church (Ephesians 5:26–27) "by the washing with water through the word, and to present her to Himself as a radiant church, without stain or wrinkle or any blemish, but holy and blameless."

Through Baptism Christ has cleansed each one of us as a priest, so that we are now declared holy and whole, pure and spotless in both body and soul before Him. And we eagerly await resurrection day, when we as priests will stand before the Lord in physical and spiritual perfection and holiness. What a blessed washing we received in Baptism! It calls us to drown daily our old Adam and live as Christ's cleansed priests. When we wash our hands and feet, we can remember our baptismal washing.

4 The Anointing Oil and Incense (30:22–38)

In verses 22–33 the Lord instructs Moses to make the sacred oil for anointing the tabernacle, its furniture, and the priests. The anointing with oil served to consecrate and make holy these objects and priests. The record of this anointing is found in Leviticus 8:10–12. In Exodus 30:34–38 the Lord instructs Moses to make the incense powder for the incense altar.

This unit helps us to understand the meaning of the word *holy*. The sacred anointing oil and the holy incense were to be totally unique, unlike any other oil or incense used in daily life. And only the priests were to be anointed with this special oil. To be "holy" then means to be "wholly (w-h-o-l-l-y) other," separated from the common and ordinary, special and unique, one of a kind.

When applied to God, the word *holy* means the one and only God, the only God who can rightfully be called God, the totally unique God. God is "wholly (w-h-o-l-l-y) other," but not in the sense of being spatially far away. After all, the holy God tabernacled in Israel's midst. Rather, God is "wholly other" in that He alone is God, totally unique and in His own category. Everything used for God's service at the tabernacle was also unique and one of a kind, separated from ordinary common life and dedicated solely to God and the tabernacle.

5 Worship Today

Consider for a moment the layout of your church building. From the entrance hall, or narthex, people enter the nave, the main room of the church building. This is much like entering the Holy Place of the tabernacle. Just as the priests entered the Holy Place, so the priesthood of all believers and those who hopefully will become part of the priesthood of all believers enter the nave.

In the front of this room is usually a railing that distinguishes between the nave and the chancel—that part of the room where we find the altar. The chancel is usually several steps higher than the nave, symbolizing reverence for the altar on which are the elements used for the Lord's Supper. The chancel is similar to the tabernacle's Most Holy Place. Usually the pastor alone serves in the chancel, from where he, as a called and ordained servant of the Word, preaches, pronounces absolution, and administers the Lord's Supper.

Now consider the furniture in the sanctuary. The baptismal font reminds us of the basin used for washing the priests. The altar reminds us of the sacrificial altar and the incense altar. Above the altar is often a cross, because the cross was the altar where Christ the High Priest offered Himself to atone for all sins. His sacrifice provided a "pleasing aroma" to God like the tabernacle's incense altar.

One also sees candlesticks, which recall the tabernacle's lampstand. Christ is the light of the world. Some churches also have a candle that remains always lit to symbolize that Christ is always the light of the world. The communion ware is often radiant gold or silver, much like the tabernacle's vessels. This points to the beauty and value of their contents, the body and blood of the Lord in, with, and under the bread and wine given to us to eat and drink.

Now consider the pastor's robes. Their purpose is not to glorify the pastor as a person but to glorify Christ and the office of the Holy Ministry, which Christ established to administer His Word and Sacraments. When the people hear the pastor pronounce absolution or preach the Word, the robes help them to hear these words as the words of the Lord and not those of Pastor Tom or Bill. Christ is speaking through the Word of God proclaimed by the pastor. And the pastor's robes, in a way similar to the Old Testament priestly robes, point our attention to the beauty of the Lord's Word and Sacraments.

When we enter the sanctuary on Sunday morning or whenever the divine service is held, we enter into the presence of the Lord. Here the Lord Jesus Christ meets us in and through His Word and Sacraments. Because the Lord meets us here through the means of grace, it is like the Tent of Meeting, where God met with His Old Testament people. Because the Lord dwells among us through the means of grace distributed here, we often call the church "the house of God." And because the holy God is here in our midst, we often call it the "sanctuary." Recall that the tent of Exodus was called the Tent of Meeting, the Lord's dwelling or tabernacle, and the sanctuary. Our very terms for the church building remind us of the Old Testament tabernacle.

During the divine service itself we are reminded that we are in the presence of the holy and majestic God. We sing during the communion service, "Holy, holy, holy Lord, God of power and might. Heaven and earth are full of Your glory." That the holy God is here should create in us a sense of deep reverence, awe, and respect. This is not an ordinary gathering like a town hall meeting or club meeting. This is a gathering of the Lord's holy people in the presence of the Holy One of Israel.

But we are also in the presence of our gracious Lord, who gave Himself for us. We come as sinners who confess their sins, just like Israel. And we receive the forgiveness of sins through absolution, the preached Word, and the Lord's Supper. That forgiveness is based on Christ's atoning sacrifice, which the tabernacle's sacrifices foreshadowed. And as the forgiven people of God, God's new Israel, we respond with praise and thanksgiving. It is a time that is heaven on earth, a time when we join with angels and archangels and all the company of heaven in praising God. What a blessed time it is! The Lord still covenants and tabernacles with His people.

6 The Artisans (31:1–11)

In these verses the Lord tells Moses He has chosen Bezalel and Oholiab to be in charge of the tabernacle's construction. The Lord endowed them and the other workers with skills to construct the tabernacle and its furnishings. They were Old Testament laborers for Christ. It reminds us that all of our abilities and skills come from the Lord and are to be used to serve Him in whatever calling He has given us.

7 The Sabbath (31:12–18)

The Lord concludes the instructions regarding the tabernacle complex with a word about the Sabbath. The Sabbath was a sign between God and the Israelites so that "you may know that I am the LORD, who makes you holy" (Exodus 31:13). The covenant made the people holy; it separated them from the other nations and made them God's people. In its rhythm of work and rest in service to God, Israel was to emulate God's pattern of creation, in which He worked six days and rested on the seventh. The Sabbath day was holy to the Lord, and it anticipated the future, when all time will be holy to the Lord.

We are no longer bound to the Sabbath day (Colossians 2:16–17). In Christ all time and space are sacred. Nevertheless, when we hear the Word and receive the Sacrament we receive a foretaste of the heavenly rest that awaits us, when we will enjoy an eternal rest with the Lord.

Concluding Activities

Speak a brief prayer, thanking God for the opportunities He gives us to worship. Make any necessary announcements and distribute study leaflet 7.

The Rupture of the Covenant

Exodus 32–33

Preparing for the Session

Central Focus

This session discusses how Israel broke the covenant and how Moses interceded. From these chapters we will learn more of Christ's role as intercessor and of the nature of Christian prayer in Christ's name.

Objectives

That the participant will be led to

1. repent of the old Adam's inclinations, which go against God and set up idols;
2. believe in the Lord Jesus Christ, who atoned for sin and intercedes for His people;
3. rejoice in the Lord's continual and gracious presence with His people on the journey to the Promised Land;
4. intend to amend his or her sinful life by the power of the Holy Spirit working through the Gospel.

Note for the small-group leaders: Lesson notes and other materials you will need begin on page 72.

For the Lecture Leader

The presenter might wish to make an overhead transparency with the lecture outline. It will help the participants to follow along during the presentation.

Session Plan

Worship

Begin the session with the hymn and prayer printed in the study leaflet. (Accompaniments are available in denominational hymnals, such as *Lutheran Worship* [refer to hymnal index], or on the *Every Voice a Song* CD set.) Continue with this devotion:

Devotion

The tragic story of the golden calf, which ruptured the covenant God made with His people, is, in a way, an age-old and continuing human experience. Fresh in Israel's memory was their deliverance from Egypt. Vividly reassuring, day and night, had been the symbol of God's presence in the pillars of cloud and fire. Nevertheless, impatient with Moses' long stay on the mountain, they ruptured the covenant, committing the most fundamental sin of all—trying to replace God. "When the people saw that Moses was so long in coming down from the mountain, they gathered around Aaron and said, 'Come, make us gods'" (Exodus 32:1).

This is the tragic history of humanity as a whole. Despite the evidence of God's grace and goodness, people try to replace God the moment they become dissatisfied with the way the Lord is running things.

It is our sin too. We need His forgiveness daily, for we continue to rupture His covenant with us. This week we have read and sung and meditated on what has been called one of the finest hymns in the English language, "Rock of Ages." It has been thought that the hymn writer drew the phrase "cleft for me" from this week's Scripture, which concludes with God's statement to Moses: "When My glory passes by, I will put you in a cleft in the rock and cover you with My hand until I have passed by" (33:22). So God provides for our forgiveness in Jesus Christ, our Rock of Ages, cleft by the soldier's spear to become our covering, our ransom, from every sin.

Lecture Presentation

Introduction

In chapters 25–31 we were with Moses on the mountaintop for 40 days and nights. The beginning of chapter 32 shifts the scene to the foot of the mountain, where the people remained during the 40 days and nights.

1 The Israelites Make a Golden Calf (32:1–6)

The people became anxious. They gathered around Aaron and insisted that he make new gods to lead them. They rejected Yahweh as their God and as the God who brought them out of Egypt. Instead, they attributed it to Moses (v. 1): "As for this fellow Moses who brought us up out of Egypt." And now Moses had abandoned them to die in the wilderness, so they claimed.

Unlike Moses, who interceded for the people and tried to correct them, Aaron gave in to their sinful demands. As he explained to Moses later (v. 22), "You know how prone these people are to evil." What a contrast in leadership! Aaron gave sinners what they wanted, but Moses admonished them, corrected the corrupt situation, and interceded for them. Not Aaron but Moses was the one who acted Christlike, like the Good Shepherd.

Aaron asked for the people's jewelry so he might fashion from it a god of gold. From this jewelry Aaron made an idol cast in the shape of a calf. Actually, the word means a "young bull." Then the people acclaimed (v. 4), "These are your gods, O Israel, who brought you up out of Egypt." The people broke the First Commandment by having other gods and by fashioning a graven image. What is worse, they attributed their salvation from Egypt to these false gods! That is the nature of unbelief, to reject the true God and to seek salvation in another god.

To attribute one's blessings and salvation to anyone or anything other than the Lord Jesus Christ is the essence of unbelief, because it gives glory to creatures rather than the Creator. The chief way to glorify the Lord is to receive His gift of forgiveness and life by faith, to let Him be your Savior and Redeemer. But unbelief says no to the Lord's gift of grace. People cannot by their own reason or strength believe in the Lord Jesus Christ or come to Him. The Holy Spirit brings people to the Lord through the Gospel. But people are able to say no to the Gospel. Divine grace and mercy are resistible. What a powerful warning this episode provides for us. St. Paul cites it and then warns us to take heed lest we fall (1 Corinthians 10:1–12).

So Aaron built an altar in front of the calf and announced (v. 5), "Tomorrow there will be a festival to the LORD." He wanted to make an either-or into a both-and, an "either the Lord *or* an idol" into "both an idol *and* the Lord." Perhaps he thought the calf symbolized the Lord or represented the Lord's throne. But Moses recognized that it was an either-or. So in verse 26 Moses says, "Whoever is for the LORD, come to me." Syncretism, that is, trying to combine the true faith with falsehood, is never acceptable to God.

In verse 6 we read that the people sacrificed whole burnt offerings and fellowship (peace) offerings and ate and drank. Does this sequence remind you of something we studied before? It parallels the covenant ratification ceremony of chapter 24. This golden calf apostasy was an anti-covenant ratification ceremony devised by sinners. The Israelites were attempting to make a new covenant with a different god! Only this one was not a holy ceremony. Instead they indulged in sinful revelry. As St. Paul also states in 1 Corinthians 10:7–8, the Hebrew word translated "revelry" means that their celebrating involved sexual sins.

2 The Lord Informs Moses (32:7–10)

However, God will not tolerate such a covenant. Either Yahweh would be Israel's God or no one would be. Either Israel would enjoy life with the Lord or it would receive death. Those are the only two options. So the Lord told Moses (v. 7), "Go down, because your people, whom you brought up out of Egypt, have become corrupt." The people's idolatry provoked the holy God to just wrath. They broke the covenant relationship by their idolatry and unbelief, and in response Yahweh disowned them. (See Matthew 10:32–33.) Yahweh called them *Moses'* people, not His.

He said (v. 9), "They are a stiff-necked people." They had been stiff-necked and stubborn ever since leaving Egypt, yet God had been "slow to anger" (34:6). But this rebellion against God brought the Lord's patience to an end and provoked God to wrath.

Therefore, God said to Moses (v. 10): "Now leave Me alone so that My anger may burn against them and that I may destroy them. Then I will make you into a great nation." God had called Moses to lead the people. And God did not want to do anything without Moses' consent. God could have simply wiped the people out on the spot, but instead He consulted with Moses. God had made Moses the mediator between God and Israel, and

God honored that. Only if Moses agreed would God destroy them.

3 Moses Intercedes (32:11–14)

Moses took the opportunity to intercede. Moses stood in the breach and would not let God destroy Israel. His prayer consisted of four parts. First (v. 11), Moses reminded Yahweh that the Israelites were Yahweh's people, whom Yahweh had brought out of Egypt. They were not Moses' people. God had made them His people, and Moses reminded God of God's commitment to them. Second, Moses argued (v. 12), What would the Egyptians say? They would conclude that Israel's God brought Israel out to destroy them, that Israel's God is a vicious and terrible God.

Third (v. 12), Moses called on God to "turn from Your fierce anger; relent and do not bring disaster on your people." The verb translated "relent" in the NIV might be translated "repent." The idiom means "to change one's mind" or "to change one's course of action." God had threatened to destroy Israel, but Moses besought God to change His mind and course of action and not to destroy them. Of course God's eternal will to save His people through grace can never be changed, but occasionally in Scripture we find the Lord graciously offering to people an opportunity to remind the Lord of His mercy and to urge Him to forgive.

Fourth (v. 10), Moses reminded God of God's promise to Abraham, Isaac, and Israel (Jacob) to make their descendants numerous and to give their descendants the Promised Land. God had said to Moses, "I will make you into a great nation." Now Moses reminded God that He had addressed those same words to Abraham (Genesis 12:2).

As a result of Moses' intercession (v. 14), "the LORD relented and did not bring on His people the disaster He had threatened." The Lord is "the compassionate and gracious God, slow to anger, abounding in love and faithfulness" (Exodus 34:6). That God turns from wrath to mercy is based on His compassionate nature (Joel 2:13; Jonah 4:2; Psalm 106:45). His ultimate will is to save and not to destroy.

Moses' prayer of intercession is rich in meaning for us. First, Moses as intercessor foreshadowed Christ Jesus, our intercessor. (Romans 8:34) "Christ Jesus, who died—more than that, who was raised to life—is at the right hand of God and is also interceding for us." Christ intercedes for us, meaning He reminds God, much like Moses did, of God's promises and of Christ's work.

4 Moses Destroys the Idol and Rebukes the Idolaters (32:15–30)

As a result of Moses' intercession, God relented and did not destroy all of Israel. But God is still the holy God. He does not tolerate idolatry. Therefore, Moses must go down to the people in order to rectify the situation and to eliminate the golden-calf idolatry. When Moses saw the idolatrous revelry of the people, he became filled with the anger of God. He broke the two stone tablets, indicating that the covenant relationship was broken. Then he took the idol, burned it, ground it to powder, scattered it on the water, and made the people drink it. Because the people wanted to worship the idol, God's judgment gave them over to their wishes and forced them to internalize their idolatry.

Next, Moses admonished Aaron. Aaron excused himself by rationalizing his actions. The sinful human nature always tries to justify itself. So Aaron said that the people pressured him into making the golden calf. His final statement is truly humorous (v. 24): "Then they gave me the gold, and I threw it into the fire, and out came this calf!" As if the golden calf made itself!

The people were still out of control and shaming the name of God, so Moses called (v. 26), "Whoever is for the LORD, come to me." All the Levites then rallied to Moses. He commanded them to go through the camp and kill the ringleaders and the most visible followers of the idolatrous worship. The Levites put to death about 3,000 people. This episode illustrates how seriously the holy God takes idolatry. It provokes God to just and holy wrath and leads to death.

After getting the situation under control and eliminating the idolatry, Moses then renewed his dialogue with God. He informed the people that because of the enormity of their sin, he had to attempt to atone for their sin. He said to them (v. 30), "Perhaps I can make atonement for your sin." It was only a "perhaps" and not automatic. God is free and cannot be manipulated or coerced. That it was only a "perhaps" revealed to the people the enormity of their apostasy against the holy God.

5 Moses Prays for the Israelites (32:31–35)

Moses then interceded for the people again. He began by confessing the people's sin (v. 31), "Oh, what a great sin these people have committed!" He did not make excuses or rationalize their sin but freely admitted it. To confess sin is to agree with God's verdict and to say back to God: Yes, You are right; we have sinned against You and deserve punishment both in this world and in hell.

Moses next pleaded for God's forgiveness for the people. If God would not forgive, Moses offered to die in the people's place (v. 32): "If not, then blot me out of the book You have written." This "book of life" is a figure of speech referring to those whom God has chosen to live with Him (Psalm 69:28; Isaiah 4:3; Daniel 12:1). The "book of life" is also mentioned in the New Testament (e.g., Revelation 20:12). It presents a beautiful picture of election—we are elected to eternal life by God's grace in Christ apart from our works.

The Lord responded to Moses by gently but firmly rejecting Moses' offer. The individuals who are impenitent idolaters will perish. Nevertheless, God promised to spare the people as a whole and to send His angel to lead them to Canaan. However, God disciplined them by sending a plague. This all reveals how seriously God takes rebellion against Him.

6 God Would Send the Israelites On without Him (33:1–6)

The Lord expanded on His previous statement to Moses. On the one hand, He remembered His promise to the patriarchs, those promises to which Moses had appealed. Israel would inherit the Promised Land. On the other hand, God distanced Himself from the sinful people by referring to them as Moses' people, whom Moses brought out of Egypt. God's angel would lead them into the Promised Land. But the holy God Himself would not go (v. 3), "because you are a stiff-necked people and I might destroy you on the way." The holy and righteous God would not tabernacle in the midst of such a stubborn and rebellious people.

And God said (v. 5), "I will decide what to do with you." The future still remained open; God's decision not to tabernacle with them was not yet final.

7 Moses Uses a "Tent of Meeting" (33:7–11)

Now there comes a parenthesis in the story. It records how Moses used to pitch a tent outside the camp where he would meet with God. We see how intimate and personal God's relationship with Moses was in verse 11: "The LORD would speak to Moses face to face, as a man speaks with his friend." Never again until the birth of Jesus was there a person who had such a close relation to God.

8 God Promises to Go with Moses (33:12–17)

Moses interceded for Israel a third time. He finally reminded God that Israel was God's people. If God loved Moses and if Israel was God's people, then it was implied that God Himself should go with Moses and the people.

God promised Moses (v. 14), "My Presence will go with you, and I will give you rest." But Moses wanted to know if this meant that God would go not only with Moses but also with the people. So Moses spoke again (v. 15), "If Your Presence does not go with us, do not send us up from here." Then Moses asked how anyone would know that God was pleased with Moses and with God's people unless God went with them. Only God's presence distinguished Moses and Israel from all other peoples. Again, God agreed for the sake of Moses (v. 17).

We learn several important things from this dialogue. First, God graciously listened to Moses and took Moses' requests seriously. God did not overpower Moses with His almighty power and majesty. Instead, He dialogued with Moses as a very personal God. God not only spoke; He also listened.

The same kind of personal relationship also holds for us. When we pray to God in Jesus' name, we are not speaking to the wall, to an implacable and cruel God. Rather, as His dear children in Christ we come before our loving Father with our petitions. And our loving Father listens to us. What a privilege it is to address God as children who speak to their loving father!

Second, what distinguished Israel from all other peoples was not Israel's great works (hardly!) or Israel's political system. Israel's only distinguishing mark was that God graciously tabernacled and went with them. The same is true for the church. What distinguishes the church from all other groups and organizations is not our good works or acts of charity. Other groups can claim that distinction as well. And the church consists of sinners like us. Rather, the distinguishing mark of the church is that the Lord Jesus Christ dwells here in our midst (Matthew 18:20), that the Lord is here forgiving us through the Gospel and Sacraments. The Lord's gracious tabernacling presence makes all the difference.

Third, the Lord agreed to go with the people only for Moses' sake. The people certainly could not claim that they deserved His abiding presence. What they deserved was only death. Yet, for Moses' sake the Lord would lead them. Again, the same is true for us. Only for Christ's sake and not because of our own worthiness does God graciously dwell with us and lead us.

9 God's Glory Passes by Moses (33:18–23)

Because God said He was pleased with Moses and knew Moses, Moses further asked to see God's glory. The Lord answered by promising to make all His goodness pass before Moses and to proclaim His name, *Yahweh.* (This event happens in the next chapter.) But Moses was to know that even he did not deserve this special experience. So Yahweh says (v. 19), "I will have mercy on whom I will have mercy, and I will have compassion on whom I will have compassion."

Moses would receive this gift only by the Lord's mercy and compassion—mercy and compassion the Lord is free to show to whom He wills. Nevertheless, even Moses could not see the Lord's face, His glory, directly, even though he had a close, personal relationship with the Lord, because no sin-riddled mortal can see God in all of His raw majesty and still live. That hope is only for those who will be as the Lord is on resurrection day (1 Corinthians 15:49–50; 1 John 3:2). For that day we all eagerly hope.

Concluding Activities

Speak a brief prayer, thanking God for being forgiving and patient with us sinners. Ask for the grace of genuine repentance. Make any necessary announcements and distribute study leaflet 8.

The Renewal of the Covenant

Exodus 34

Preparing for the Session

Central Focus

This session concerns God's renewal of the broken covenant. It will focus especially on the revelation of God's nature and character.

Objectives

That the participant will be led to

1. repent of his or her rebellious sinful nature;
2. believe in the forgiveness that comes from God's graciousness in Christ;
3. rejoice in God's grace and compassion;
4. wholeheartedly love and trust in the Lord above all.

Note for the small-group leaders: Lesson notes and other materials you will need begin on page 75.

Session Plan

Worship

Begin the session with the hymn printed in the study leaflet. (Accompaniments are available in denominational hymnals, such as *Lutheran Worship* [refer to hymnal index], or on the *Every Voice a Song* CD set.) Follow with this devotion:

Devotion

Rembrandt's famous painting of Moses holding the Ten Commandments, dated 1659, depicts the commandments engraved in golden letters on black stone. That Rembrandt had the scene of the second giving of the commandments in mind—after Israel's idolatry—is evident in how he paints Moses with a glowing, radiant face.

Michelangelo also portrayed Moses' bright moment in God's presence. Aware that the Hebrew word for "shone," as with beams or rays of light, could also mean in Hebrew "horns," Michelangelo carved his statue of Moses with animal horns protruding from Moses' forehead. The statue stands in the Church of St. Peter in Chains in Rome. The awareness that "horns" in the Old Testament also denotes power permeates the statue, as Moses with one powerful hand holds the tables of the Law and with the other plays with his long beard. The statue fairly breathes strength of will and great dignity.

It is fair for us to imagine ourselves, like Moses, radiant with God's glory when we hold aloft God's commandments. Our lives, too, become powerful, as the Spirit works within us through the Word of God when we witness concerning God, our hope, our purpose, our goal.

We could carry our identification with this statue of Moses a little further, as we see ourselves confidently "stroking the long beard" of the full life God gives us. A life in tune with God is possible only because of Jesus Christ, our hope and goal. He erases not one "jot or tittle" of the Law, but He fulfills its demands for us. This strengthens our life with genuine purpose. Be sure to keep this portrayal of yourself in mind as you discuss this section of God's Word this week.

Conclude with the prayer printed in the study leaflet.

Lecture Presentation

Introduction

In the previous two chapters we saw how Israel broke the covenant by worshiping the golden calf. Israel's idolatry provoked God to wrath. God reveals His grace by being willing to listen to Moses. And Moses showed his great love for the people as he pleaded for them in spite of their faithlessness and rebellion.

At the end of chapter 33 Moses asked to see the Lord's glory. In chapter 34 Yahweh fulfills His promise and passes in front of Moses.

1 A New Set of Stone Tablets (34:1–4)

Moses had broken the first set of stone tablets containing the ten words, indicating that the covenant had been broken. Now the Lord instructed Moses to chisel out two more tablets, on which the Lord would write the ten words of the first set. This instruction reveals that God would renew His covenant with Israel. The Lord then summoned Moses to ascend the mountain once again.

2 The Lord's Appearance before Moses (34:5–7)

While Moses was on the mountain, Yahweh passed in front of Moses as He had promised and made the proclamation of verses 6–7. This event is one of the highlights of the entire book and, in fact, of the entire Bible. Here God reveals Himself, His name, and His character. It is such an important revelation that it is worth studying closely. It reveals to Moses and to us what kind of God the Lord is.

People often have the idea that the God of the Old Testament is a cruel, vicious, and spiteful God, while the God of the New Testament is gracious and loving. Nothing could be further from the truth! Our God who has revealed Himself in Christ is the same God who revealed Himself to Abraham and Moses. When we read about God in the Old Testament, we are reading about our God, who has made us members of His one people in Christ. Our God is the same God who revealed Himself to Moses in Exodus 34.

What kind of God is that? We have seen how God is the holy God who was provoked to anger by Israel's idolatry. He is not one to trifle with or to treat lightly. Nevertheless, God is not by nature an angry and wrathful God. He did not ultimately want to destroy Israel. God does not desire the death of anyone. "Do I take any pleasure in the death of the wicked? declares the sovereign LORD. Rather, am I not pleased when they turn from their ways and live?" (Ezekiel 18:23). In Exodus 34 God reveals to Moses what He is like deep down inside; deep within His heart is only compassion, grace, and love.

When God passed before Moses, He proclaimed (vv. 6–7): "The LORD, the LORD, the compassionate and gracious God, slow to anger, abounding in love and faithfulness, maintaining love to thousands, and forgiving wickedness, rebellion and sin." God begins by pronouncing His name, "Yahweh" (translated "the LORD"). Old Testament names were not simply neutral labels or tags, such as "Bill" or "Betty" today. Rather, one's name revealed one's character and nature. To know the name of another person was to know that person's character; it was to really know that person. To call on "Yahweh" is to call on the one who said in 3:14, "I AM WHO I AM" (or "I will be what I will be").

In 34:6 God reveals Himself as Yahweh, who is "the compassionate and gracious God." God is very compassionate and tenderhearted. And He shows grace toward sinners. God's grace is His undeserved and unmerited favor toward sinners. Sinners deserve and merit only God's just wrath, but instead God in Christ makes His face shine on them. He looks on them with favor; He shows grace toward them.

The next phrase says that Yahweh is "slow to anger." This means He is patient and not easily provoked to anger. Very often humans are quick to anger, hotheaded and ill-tempered. We "fly off the handle," are irrational and out of control. But God is not like that; He is "slow to anger." We can see this throughout the Old Testament.

God does not immediately and without warning destroy sinners in His wrath. He gave the world time to repent during the days of Noah. He gave the Canaanites over 400 years before Joshua conquered the land. He constantly warned the Israelites through His prophets before He took them into exile. He warned Egypt through Moses and the plagues before He killed the firstborn. He warned Nineveh through Jonah and gave the city 40 days to repent. When Nineveh did repent, God relented and spared them (Jonah 3:10).

God is "slow to anger." In fact, Judgment Day has not yet come because (2 Peter 3:9) God "is patient with you, not wanting anyone to perish, but everyone to come to repentance."

On the one hand, God is "slow to anger"; on the other hand, God is (v. 6) "abounding in love and faithfulness." He does not abound in anger but in love. The word translated "love" in the New International Version is sometimes translated "steadfast love" or "mercy." It is the word that occurs in the verse repeated throughout Psalm 136: "Give thanks to the LORD, for He is good. His love endures forever." Whereas God's wrath has a beginning when it is provoked and caused by human sin, His mercy and love are from eternity (Psalm 103:17). His love precedes all human works and is not caused by them. God's acts of mercy are caused by and flow from His own compassionate and gracious heart. He abounds in love.

The passage adds that the Lord abounds in faithfulness. For the sake of God's promises to Abraham, Isaac, Jacob, and Moses, God would go with Israel to Canaan. The passage goes on by stating that Yahweh maintains love to thousands. Perhaps a better translation would be that He maintains love to the thousandth generation (Deuteronomy 7:9)—that is, an unlimited number of people and generations.

God's undeserved love created the covenant in the first place, and it continues to undergird and maintain it.

All of this issues in the forgiveness of sins (v. 7): "and forgiving wickedness, rebellion and sin." Only on the basis of forgiveness did Israel still have a life and a future.

What an amazing and wonderful revelation of God this is! The passage is worth memorizing because it is so important. In fact, it became almost a creed for ancient Israel, as it is quoted often in the Old Testament. How unlike us God is! How often we are quick to anger—to a selfish anger, not a holy and just anger, and lacking in compassion. How often we bear a grudge and refuse to forgive! How often we are coldhearted and unloving! But God is a "compassionate and gracious God, slow to anger, abounding in love and faithfulness." He shows mercy even toward those who went after other gods and rejected Him.

It is quite clear what God would have been justified in doing on the basis of His Law. The sinful idolatry was deliberate, blatant, inexcusable. The whole people deserved to die. Yet, the amazing thing is that God is much more eager to forgive than to condemn, to be gracious than to destroy. This is truly amazing grace!

So often we are tempted to yawn in boredom when we hear the message of God's grace in Christ and when we receive divine forgiveness. We expect it and assume it. We think to ourselves, "Pastor, tell me something I don't know. Give me some principles for Christian living and some practical how-to's, but don't always tell me of God's grace. Of course God forgives me. That's His job!" When we presume God's grace, we need to be reminded once again of what we really deserve and of what God had every right to have done. God does not owe us grace as if we deserve it. Quite the contrary, by nature we are no better than the ancient Israelites. We deserve and merit nothing but death and wrath.

Divine grace is certainly amazing and startling. Yet, we can firmly rely on it and stake our lives on it. It accords with the depths of God's inner being. When a friend acts strangely and not in a way that corresponds with what we have come to know about that person, we often say, "You are not yourself today." When God shows mercy and saves, He is acting "like Himself" and is doing what He prefers to do.

Unfortunately, the human heart is so perverse and perverted that it often misinterprets God's slowness to anger and His abundant love as indulgence and toleration of sin. God does truly forgive, but He does not permissively tolerate those who continually persist in sin, those who say no to His grace. In Jeremiah 30:11 and 46:28 this sentence applies to God's disciplinary and corrective chastisement. Just as loving parents forgive a disobedient child but also chastise in order to correct the child, so God chastises. But His punishment lasts only to the third and fourth generation, whereas His love outweighs and surpasses His punishment, because it endures to the thousandth generation.

3 Moses' Intercession (34:8–9)

On the basis of Yahweh's self-disclosure as a gracious and forgiving God, Moses intercedes once again: "O LORD, if I have found favor in Your eyes . . . then let the LORD go with us. Although this is a stiff-necked people, forgive our wickedness and our sin, and take us as Your inheritance." Moses prayed this while bowing down to the ground and worshiping. Moses' response to God's gracious character is humble gratitude and worship.

Moses acknowledged that the people are "a stiff-necked people." Yet he prayed for the Lord's presence and forgiveness, based solely on the Lord's mercy. Because of God's grace in Christ Jesus, and not at all because of our character, He will abide with us and forgive us. His mercy in Christ is our only basis of appeal.

4 The Lord's Answer (34:10–14)

The Lord answered Moses' prayer in the affirmative on the basis of His mercy. The Lord promised to do wonders in the sight of the people. These wonders and awesome deeds included driving out the people who inhabited the Promised Land.

However, this generation of Israelites would benefit from the promise only by faith. Such faith produces a life in accord with God's instructions. Therefore, the Lord warned them not to make a covenant with the idolatrous peoples in the land lest they become a snare for God's people. Rather, Israel should destroy the land's idols and altars.

In verse 14 Yahweh says, "Do not worship any other god, for the LORD, whose name is Jealous, is a jealous God." Yahweh alone is God, and He insists on that. He will not share His bride with other lovers or gods.

5 Israel in the Land (34:15–26)

In this section the Lord gives instructions that do not represent a new and different Decalogue, because verse 28 records that the Lord wrote the original ten words on the new stone tablets (see v. 1). Rather, these instructions state what the Lord wanted to particularly emphasize to Israel. Many of them are the same as those given in chapter 23, which concern the festivals Israel was to keep. They focus on the First and Third Commandments.

If the Israelites recently made an idol while all alone in the wilderness at Sinai, what would they do in the land of Canaan, where all the inhabitants were idolaters? The temptation toward reverting to idolatry would become too strong for them. Therefore, God repeats His instruction that the Israelites should not make a covenant with the inhabitants of the land (v. 15; see 23:29–30). If they intermarried with the idolaters, they would soon become idolatrous themselves (v. 16). The concern was not to maintain some sort of racial purity. Rather, God was concerned that Israel remain faithful to Him alone. It was a religious concern.

We Christians live in the world. Nevertheless, we Christians are not of the world. We, like ancient Israel, are called to resist idolatry and falsehood and to remain faithful to our Lord and Savior.

In verses 18–26, the Lord expands on the sacred festivals that He mentioned in 23:14–19. Included were the Feast of Ingathering or Tabernacles held in the fall, the Feast of Unleavened Bread—Passover—held in the early spring, the Feast of Weeks or Pentecost held seven weeks later, and the Sabbath day.

The Promised Land would be a land flowing with milk and honey, a bountiful land where the Lord would bless them with crops, cattle, and children. In response and out of gratitude to their gracious Lord, the Israelites were to offer the firstfruits of their crops and the firstborn of their cattle to the Lord. Their firstborn sons were to be "redeemed." All of Israel and all of their crops and cattle belonged to the Lord. To acknowledge this, they were to give the Lord the first of what they had received.

The Old Testament Promised Land foreshadowed the new and greater Promised Land that we will all inherit. It will be an abundant and bountiful land, a new Garden of Eden, a new creation that no longer moans in pain (Romans 8:19–22; Revelation 22).

6 Moses' Radiant Face (34:27–35)

Verse 28 tells us that Moses fasted while remaining on the mountain 40 days and nights. This period was in addition to the 40 days and nights that Moses remained earlier before the golden-calf apostasy. Again, we see how much Moses loved his people, to such an extent that he fervently interceded and fasted for 40 days and nights.

When Moses came down from Mount Sinai, his face was radiant because he had spoken with the Lord. Moses then assembled the people, who were afraid to come near him, and he gave them all the instructions from God. After speaking, Moses veiled his face, but whenever he entered the tent to speak with the Lord, he removed the veil. For the sake of Moses, the Lord renewed the covenant. That special status was revealed to the people by Moses' radiant face. Moses' radiant face reflected the radiant glory of the Lord. And it anticipated another transfiguration, the transfiguration of Christ, who is the new and greater covenant mediator.

Concluding Activities

Speak a brief prayer, thanking God for His forgiveness and patience with us. Praise Him for His love and grace. Make any necessary announcements and distribute study leaflet 9.

The Building of the Tabernacle

Exodus 35–40

Preparing for the Session

Central Focus

This session is based on chapters 35–40, which report how the tabernacle complex was made and erected. Special attention will be given to the significance of the overall layout, to the Lord's tabernacling presence, and to God's people as a pilgrim people.

Objectives

That the participant will be led to

1. acknowledges the unholy and sinful nature of all people;
2. receive by faith the forgiveness and holiness only Christ Jesus gives;
3. rejoice that the Lord graciously tabernacles with His people;
4. understand more fully what it means to be Christ's holy and pilgrim people;
5. dedicate his or her abilities and possessions in service to the Lord Jesus Christ by the power of the Holy Spirit working through the Gospel;
6. eagerly await the second advent of the Lord, when all space and time will be filled with His holiness.

Note for the small-group leaders: Lesson notes and other materials you will need begin on page 78.

Session Plan

Worship

Begin the session with the hymn printed in the study leaflet. (Accompaniments are available in denominational hymnals, such as *Lutheran Worship* [refer to hymnal index], or on the *Every Voice a Song* CD set.) Follow the hymn with the prayer printed in the study leaflet.

Lecture Presentation

Introduction

These chapters must be understood in light of the previous narrative. According to the Law all of idolatrous Israel should have been destroyed on the spot. That would have been the end of the book of Exodus with no tabernacle. But the Gospel has the last word over the Law, and therefore the story continues. Only by virtue of the Lord's undeserved and lavish grace does the Lord allow Israel to live and to build the tabernacle, and then He graciously chooses to dwell in the tabernacle (40:34–38). Here we see the fulfillment of this course's subtitle: The Lord covenants (again!) and tabernacles with His people.

Much of the account repeats verbatim what is given in chapters 25–31 about how to build the tabernacle and its furnishings. In these six chapters we read how the divine instructions were carried out exactly as given. At the end of chapter 39 comes the summary statement (vv. 42–43): "The Israelites had done all the work just as the LORD had commanded Moses. Moses inspected the work and saw that they had done it just as the LORD had commanded. So Moses blessed them."

What does this obedience mean? At the very least we can say that the Israelites certainly learned their lesson! But far more was involved. This obedience gives evidence of their profound gratitude to God for graciously sparing and forgiving them. They were so overjoyed and thankful that the Lord forgave them that they happily followed the Lord's instructions. They did not murmur and complain, but they wholeheartedly and with joy built the tabernacle. Faith bears fruit.

1 Materials Are Gathered and Artisans Selected (35:1–36:7)

Further evidence of their profound gratitude is provided by the way they freely contributed. All the people brought freewill offerings "morning after morning" (36:3) in such abundance that they had to be "restrained from bringing more, because what they already had was more than enough to do all the work" (36:6–7).

The whole scene is truly a marvel. The same people who had brought their gold to make an idol were now bringing their gold, treasures, and talents to build the Lord's tabernacle. The same people who had used their God-given treasures and talents to worship their own creation were now using them to worship the Divine Giver.

That is the radical change that the Gospel of the Lord's grace produces. It makes a new creation. It changes stone-cold idolatrous hearts into thankful believing hearts that serve the Lord.

We, too, like ancient Israel, were once "by nature objects of wrath. But because of His great love for us, God, who is rich in mercy, made us alive with Christ even when we were dead in transgressions—it is by grace you have been saved" (Ephesians 2:3–5). Through Baptism we died to sin and were raised with Christ to life. As new creatures the Lord now calls us to serve Him with our time, talents, and treasures. Just as Israel earlier provided a sinful example that we are warned to avoid, so now Israel gives us a God-pleasing example to follow.

2 The Tabernacle Complex Is Constructed (36:8–40:33)

This section describes how the Israelites made the tabernacle, its curtains and furniture, and the priestly garments. Chapter 40 records how Moses then followed the Lord's instructions and set up the tabernacle structure. That Moses erected the structure reveals his continuing and unique role of covenant mediator. Moses wraps into one the roles of prophet, priest, and king, and as such he foreshadows Christ Jesus.

The one feature of the tabernacle we have not yet examined is its overall layout and plan. The tabernacle complex was set in the middle of the camp of Israel. The Lord was to be the center of Israel's life not only spiritually but even geographically. Some towns in North America and Europe were designed with the church building, with its towering steeple, located at their center. What a beautiful picture! It indicates what Israel was truly to be and how the Lord considered it—not simply as a political nation but as an assembly of believers gathered around and by the Lord's gracious presence and means of grace. The true nature of ancient Israel was a church before Christ. Israel found its identity only in the Lord's gracious covenant and tabernacling with them (33:14–17).

The same holds for the Lord's people after Christ. The church finds her identity and nature only in the Lord Jesus Christ, in whom the fullness of God tabernacles among us, only in the Lord's presence and gifts given us through the Gospel and the Sacraments.

When we begin to think of our congregation as simply another voluntary association of likeminded people, as simply another civic-service club, thinking about the tabernacle's location in the middle of Israel's camp can help correct us. We are the new Israel gathered around the gracious presence of the Lord. In fact, the New Testament calls the church the temple of God. What an exalted status the Lord Jesus Christ has given us poor sinners! We are His temple!

Around the tabernacle's courtyard were encamped the 12 tribes of Israel. Between the tribes and the courtyard fence were encamped the Levites.

The tabernacle was divided into two rooms, with the Most Holy Place measuring a perfect cube 15 by 15 by 15 feet. The tent's opening, which faced east, was located in the middle of the outer courtyard. This put the Most Holy Place in the middle of the courtyard's western half, with 30 feet to the east (which was the Holy Place) and to the west (which was courtyard). In the middle of the courtyard's eastern half stood the bronze sacrificial altar, and between it and the tent stood the bronze basin.

This overall layout reveals several significant features. First, it was oriented toward the east: the courtyard gate was on the eastern end and the tent opened to the east. Why east? Because the sun rises in the east, and therefore, at early dawn shone upon the dwelling place of God, displaying its beauty.

Second, the whole complex corresponds to a very symmetrical pattern. The courtyard was twice as long as it was wide. The entrance into the Holy Place stood in the middle of the courtyard. In the middle of the courtyard's eastern half was the sacrificial altar. In the middle of its western half was the Most Holy Place with the ark in the center.

This symmetry revealed a well-ordered and harmonious creation of God. When God first created the heavens and earth, He created a well-structured and orderly creation.

Everything was given its proper place and function so that God saw that it was good (Genesis 1). But with Adam and Eve's fall into sin, the creation itself "was subjected to frustration" and has been groaning in travail ever since (Romans 8:19–22). Yet, God set up the tabernacle complex, His dwelling place, to be harmoniously ordered. As such it represented a miniature creation, a foretaste and down payment of the new creation, when all creation will be restored to perfect harmony. And in the middle sections of this miniature creation stood the two most important items—the ark and the sacrificial altar. Everything else was built around these two. Just as the tree of life stood in the center of the Garden of Eden, so the two places where God gives life were in the center of the tabernacle.

Third, although God dwelt with Israel, there was still a distance and an inapproachability. The Levites camped between the courtyard and the Israelite tribes, thus forming a kind of protective buffer zone. The courtyard fence or curtain was 7½ feet high, so no profane eyes could see the holy ceremonies. Only the Aaronic priests could approach the tent and serve at the sacrificial altar. (Numbers 3:38) "Anyone else who approached the sanctuary was to be put to death." Only the high priest could enter the Most Holy Place and only once a year (Leviticus 16).

All of this reveals that only holy people can stand before the holy God. Only holy priests can approach the Holy One of Israel. The sinful Israelites did not have direct access to God. Mediators were necessary, and distance had to be maintained. In the Old Testament there were degrees of holiness. In terms of people we see the ranking: high priest—priests—Levites—Israelites—unclean Gentiles. Parallel to that are the degrees of holy space: Most Holy Place—Holy Place—courtyard—Levitical camp—Israelite tribal camps—the wilderness.

But in Christ the boundaries are removed; with His death the curtain is torn. Through Baptism even we Gentiles have been made holy priests, so that we can confidently "enter the Most Holy Place by the blood of Jesus" (Hebrews 10:19). Christ has elevated us all to the level of holy priests, with Him as our High Priest. Through Him we are all one and all have direct access to God. Now, where Christ is—in His Word and Sacraments—there is holy space. The Old Testament tabernacle helps clarify for us what rich treasures and what an exalted status the Lord has given us.

Nevertheless, even now we have access to the Lord Jesus Christ and through Him to God the Father only in a mediate way, that is, only through the means of grace—His Word (written and spoken) and His holy Sacraments of Baptism and the Lord's Supper. Apart from these means we have no access to the gracious God. But we are given the hope that on the Last Day Christ "will transform our lowly bodies so that they will be like His glorious body" (Philippians 3:21). Then "we shall see Him as He is" (1 John 3:2), directly and immediately. Then all of creation, all space and time, will be filled with His glory. What a blessed hope that is!

3 The Tabernacle Is Filled with God's Glory (40:34–38)

After Moses set up the tabernacle complex, "the cloud covered the Tent of Meeting, and the glory of Yahweh filled the tabernacle" (v. 34). For the moment the cloud and the glory of Yahweh filled the whole tent, so that even Moses could not enter. Later the cloud would rest only above the ark (Leviticus 16:2).

We have seen this cloud before. It is the pillar of cloud and the pillar of fire that led the Israelites out of Egypt (Exodus 13:21–22; 14:19–20; 16:10) and that rested on the top of Mount Sinai (Exodus 19). It is the cloud that Moses entered while on the mountain 40 days and nights (24:15–18). The same cloud appeared at Moses' private tent outside the camp when Moses met with the Lord (33:7–11). And the Lord came down in the cloud on Mount Sinai when He revealed Himself to Moses as "Yahweh, the compassionate and gracious God" (34:5–7).

God actually located His presence in the cloud. The phrase "the glory of the Lord" refers to both the splendor of the fiery cloud and the actual presence of the Lord in the cloud. With this glory-cloud the Lord revealed His presence to the people so that they could see it. Yet, at the same time, the Lord concealed Himself with this cloud, since no mortal can see the Lord in all of His naked majesty and brilliance and still live.

The same duality of revealing and concealing carries over into the New Testament. The baby in Bethlehem's manger, who grew up in Nazareth and walked through Palestine, who hung on the cross is God Himself, God Incarnate. Yet He concealed His full majesty during His state of humiliation. And now in the Gospel and the

Sacraments the Lord continues to be present with us though in a hidden form. Yet we look forward to the day when "we shall see Him as He is" (1 John 3:2).

The book of Exodus ends with the note that the glory-cloud led the Israelites in all their travels. The Lord did not stay on Mount Sinai. He graciously tabernacled with His people throughout their journey. He fulfilled His promise given to Moses in chapters 33–34 that He would go with the people. The ultimate fulfillment comes in Jesus Christ. (John 1:14) "The Word became flesh and made His dwelling among us." The Lord Jesus Christ continues to go with us.

But not only with us. The glory-cloud led the Israelites on their journey. And where did the Lord lead them? To Canaan, the Promised Land. The people of God are a pilgrim people who journey through the wilderness to the Promised Land. And in this journey they are led by the Lord. So also the new Israel. We live in the world but "our citizenship is in heaven" (Philippians 3:20). "I'm but a stranger here, heaven is my home," we sing in a familiar hymn. Life in this world is a life filled with danger and temptation. So many troubles and trials daily confront us. So many enemies try to destroy us and deprive us of eternal life, not only flesh and blood but Satan and his powers. Life in this fallen world is a life under the cross, a life of being persecuted and ridiculed for the faith, a life that makes us anxious.

But life under the cross is life under a glorious cross, the cross of Christ the Lord, the cross where He offered Himself up for us and by which He made us His Israel. The Lord truly does covenant and tabernacle with His people. And that Lord, who is all for us, leads us during our journey through this wilderness. He protects us from our foes, provides for us on the way, and guides us. Where is He leading us? To the new and better Promised Land, the Holy Land where the Holy Lord will dwell with His holy people. There we will find rest from the weary journey. With the Lord in the lead, that is a journey worth traveling. Lead Thou on, dear Lord Jesus!

Concluding Activities

If possible, announce the next LifeLight course and encourage participants to register and invite others to participate also. Speak a prayer thanking God for the growth experienced during this course and continued growth through His Word for all participants.

Small-Group Leaders Material

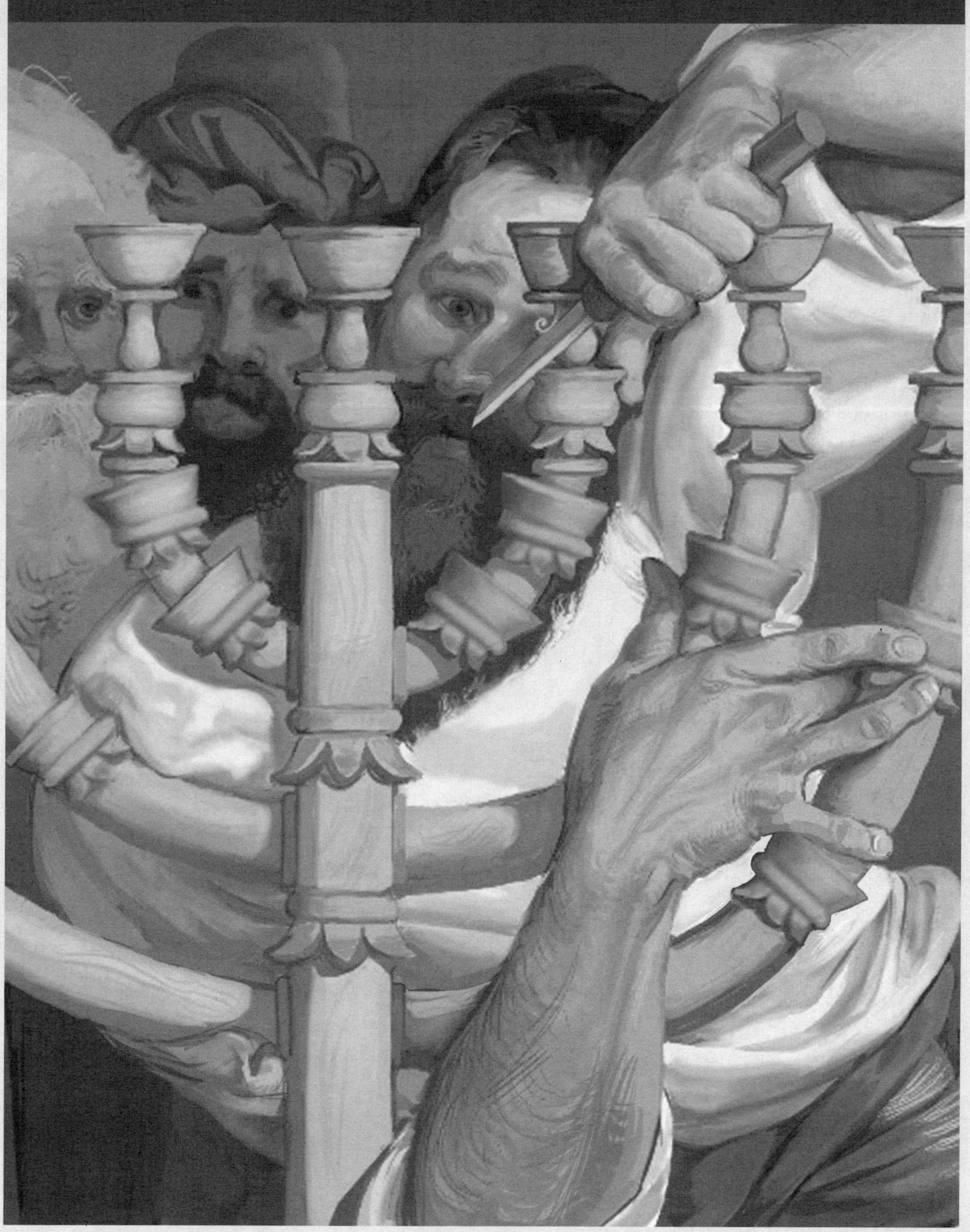

The Ten Words of the Covenant

Exodus 20:1–20

Preparing for the Session

Central Focus

This introductory session ties Exodus, Part 2 with Exodus, Part 1 and discusses the ten words or commandments.

Objectives

That the participant will be led to

1. repent of failure to keep the Law of God;
2. believe in the forgiveness of sins in Christ Jesus;
3. rejoice in the deliverance from bondage the Lord has given;
4. willingly and gladly follow the instructions of God's Law as one who is empowered by the Spirit working through the Gospel.

For the Small-Group Leader

LifeLight divides Exodus into two Bible studies. The division is hardly arbitrary. You should know and appreciate how neatly the two Bible studies revolve around Exodus 20:2. That which follows Exodus 20:2 is strongly based on that which has come before God's declaration in this verse: "I am the LORD your God, who brought you out of Egypt, out of the land of slavery."

Four verbs summarize that which preceded 20:2 and that which follows. These are the verbs in the subtitles of the two courses: "The Lord *Calls* and *Delivers* His People" and "The Lord *Covenants* and *Tabernacles* with His People." While this course deals with the second title, keep in mind what has gone before in Exodus, as expressed in the first title. You will want to tie in with the first 19 chapters. Encourage participants to review the events of the first 19 chapters. The four verbs—*calls, delivers, covenants, tabernacles*—are prominent in the study leaflets.

Participants will likely understand easily how *call* and *deliver* describe God's relationship to Israel. However, the very familiarity of these verbs may cause some to overlook important concepts behind them and their application to life today. God—not Moses or Israel—is the main figure in Exodus. We may easily forget that, especially if our knowledge of the exodus has been colored by the portrayal of Moses by Charlton Heston in the popular movie *The Ten Commandments.* Also, the exodus theme in Israeli national life today promotes a focus on Israel itself.

But, actually, it is always God who calls us to Himself; it is not that we seek "to touch the face of God" or climb the ladder to heaven rung by rung by our pious thoughts and contemplation. God's action is a central theme in all of sacred Scripture, certainly also in Exodus, and we dare not overlook or minimize that it is God who calls and we who respond.

Similarly, God's deliverance of Israel must not focus entirely on Israel's deliverance from slavery in Egypt. God delivers Israel, not just to rescue them from slavery but to call Israel to be His people, with all that that entails. Peter, in his first epistle, describes how God has delivered us from slavery to sin as he speaks of how we have been "called . . . out of darkness into His marvelous light" (1 Peter 2:9). Proper emphasis on God's deliverance and His making us what we are defuses our tendency to make our response a way of "playing ball" with God. As a practical people, we often want religion to work for us with obvious success. An emphasis on what God does constantly for us should also contribute to the breakdown of the wall of "cheap grace."

The verbs *covenant* and *tabernacle,* despite their strangeness to most modern ears, get beyond an easy and perhaps even trite way of thinking about God living within us or having Jesus in our hearts. We will consider the great depth of meaning for the Jew—and for us too—behind those verbs. We will stretch our imaginations as we attempt to see meaning behind the details of the covenant and of the tabernacle, with their striking application to the life of God's people in today's world also. Hopefully we will discover the more unfamiliar second half of the book as a gold mine of valuable details that, possibly heretofore undiscovered, now will enrich our lives.

Small-Group Discussion Helps

This first lesson holds what may be the most familiar portion of Scripture to people both within and without the Christian church. Accordingly, as discussion leader in your small group, you face a nearly impossible task of covering the Ten Commandments as thoroughly as you and group members may want. Be sure to emphasize the most vital points of each day's questions. You need to hear what members of the group are saying and asking and not worry about covering every detail the Ten Commandments speak to.

Day 1 • Exodus 20:1–6

1. Typically, people react to the Ten Commandments as rules and regulations, either as impossible to keep and therefore to be ignored or given up on or as a challenge to be met for getting God on one's side. The comment quoted in the question would seem to imply that the Ten Commandments are a simple recipe unnecessarily complicated by politicians.

2. **Challenge question.** Encourage participants to state how the Law of God works in their own lives as curb, mirror, and rule. (a) Paul refers to how God wrote His law on the human heart. This inward knowledge of right and wrong, as well as the way in which God's Law is enforced by the laws and rules that govern us in everyday life, discourages and punishes wrongdoing and preserves civilized behavior. In this way God's Law curbs, or controls, the influence of sin in the world. (b) God's Law reveals sin for what it is—rebellion against God. Paul notes that God's Law exposes coveting as the root of sinful behavior, not just innocent daydreaming. In the mirror of the Ten Commandments we see ourselves as we truly are, in need of God's forgiveness and direction, in need, therefore, of Jesus Christ and the forgiveness and strength He provides for us. (c) God's Word instructs the person who loves God and desires to please Him concerning what is in line with God's will and what is out of line with His will. Like a light, God's Law illuminates the pathway of the God-pleasing life. As rule, the commandments help us find our way through the maze of life.

3. "Your God" makes God most personal to us. "Other gods before Me" reminds us that ancient peoples had many gods. Actually, we could say that people today are little different in that they give many ideals, persons, or objects the honor, obedience, and faith that should be given only to God. We do well, in our understanding of the commandments, to keep in front of each commandment God's opening declaration: "I am the LORD your God." Defining "jealous" gives opportunity to emphasize the power of words and our need to define them adequately in their context. Envy is not to be emphasized here but vigilance in guarding a possession. We are God's possession. He is 100 percent concerned about us. That makes Him zealous about our welfare and intolerant of unfaithfulness toward Him, which contributes to our harm.

4. (a) Actually, idolatry generally comes down to a worship of ourselves. We are ready to worship at any altar if it promises to give us what we want for ourselves. Satan promised Eve, "You will be like God" (Genesis 3:5). We still find that promise appealing; it is the essence of sin. (b) *For personal reflection. Sharing optional.* This is a question of introspection. Encourage your group to be open enough to describe some of the gods they carve through their attitudes, drives, and deeds. Move cautiously, however. Some may not be capable of being so open; some may need more time.

Day 2 • Exodus 20:7–11

5. (a) Ps. 135:13 tells us that God's name reveals Him as the one who is forever, whose renown is told throughout history, as one generation tells the next of what God has done and how glorious and wonderful He is. (b) Psalm 148:13 urges us to praise and exalt God's name. God's name reveals Him as the one whose "splendor is above the earth and the heavens." (c) Isaiah 57:15 declares that God's name is holy; He lives in a high and lofty place, far removed from us sinners. Yet God is also merciful and compassionate and reaches down in mercy to contrite sinners. (d) Matthew 1:21 tells us that the name of Jesus reveals His mission: to save sinners. The name *Jesus* comes from a Hebrew phrase that means "the Lord saves." (e) Matthew 1:23 recalls the prophecy concerning Jesus spoken through Isaiah, that the Savior would be "Immanuel"—from a Hebrew phrase that means "God is

with us." In this way also the Lord's name tells us that He is our Savior.

6. (a) When we use this curse, we are asking God to condemn someone or something and to consign the object of our cursing to eternal punishment in hell. (b) When we swear in this way, we are calling on God to attest that what we say is the truth and to punish us if we are failing to tell the absolute truth. (c) When we curse or swear, we are using God's holy name thoughtlessly and uselessly—or worse, we are presumptuously commanding God to punish others or us. At the very least we are being careless with God's name; at worst we are placing ourselves above God. In both cases, we are committing a terrible sin. To call down God's judgment on anyone—cursing—is always wrong. To swear, as testifying in court to tell the truth, is not prohibited. But swearing falsely or uselessly profanes God's name.

7. (a) What we must emphasize with this question is that *holy* means more than "pure" or "perfect," as we speak colloquially about the "holier than thou" attitude. Rather, we are a "holy people," not because we are better than others, but because we are forgiven and therefore separated by God from the unredeemed to be God's possession. All the days of the week belong to God, but one is given special significance. On the seventh day of the week God rested from His work of creation to contemplate what He had done and what He would do in bringing His people to Himself for the eternal Sabbath. (b) Questions may arise about why Christians worship on Sunday or if Christians are obliged to rest on Sunday as Jews were commanded to rest on the Sabbath. Jesus' fulfillment of the ceremonial law canceled this part of the commandment (Matthew 12:1–13; Colossians 2:16–17). Instead, Christians freely choose to worship on Sunday to celebrate and commemorate the resurrection of Jesus on the first day of the week. (c) Encourage members of your discussion group to say how they set aside time for worship and for reading or hearing God's Word each week. Most often, probably, this will involve Sunday school and church attendance. But this may not always occur on Sundays, especially in the case of those who must work on at least some Sundays. Special customs or personal practices may also be mentioned as a way of observing time for worship and listening to the Lord.

Day 3 • Exodus 20:12–14

8. (a) God promises to bless the keeping of the commandment to honor parents with a long tenure in the land God would give them. (b) The apostle Paul observes that this is the first commandment to which God attached a promise to bless those who kept it. (c) Families comprise the basic unit of human society, and when this unit is sound and solid, with healthy relationships existing within the family, a society of people has a secure foundation on which to build other units. On the other hand, where families are characterized by disintegration, where children do not receive sound training in their early years, and where parental authority suffers, no other social units can flourish either. Sound families, where children are nurtured and parents are respected, result in more moral, secure, industrious, and prosperous communities and nations.

9. (a) Under the commandment to protect and preserve life Jesus included actions that embitter or threaten to shorten life in any way. Among these actions are anger that desires to do harm and a contemptuous, demeaning attitude. (b) Some may maintain that respect for human life has grown and may cite a keener public conscience, at least within many nations, concerning such issues as the protection of human rights through law, condemnation of the torture of prisoners, concern for the health of poor and disadvantaged people, and humanitarian aid to victims of war and national disasters. But others may cite factors to indicate a decreasing value of human life even in so-called civilized nations: a widespread acceptance of abortion; a growing tolerance of euthanasia; disregard for public safety both by individuals (as evidenced by the use of alcohol and drugs) and by corporations (as evidenced by abuse of our environment); abuse of children, spouses, and the elderly; and apathy toward the plight of victims of criminal violence. You could add to the examples given here, but every example should be framed by the overall principle "You shall not murder." This command does not prohibit capital punishment or the waging of war by governments, which exist as God's agents to preserve order in the world. Murder refers to a deliberate and premeditated act that takes place outside the law. The commandment forbids loss of life inflicted by illegal means.

10. The verb on which the prohibition of the Sixth Commandment rests is used exclusively in the Old Testament to describe marital infidelity or adultery, not fornication. So the real concern of this commandment is the sacredness of marriage, thus dealing with the family as a social unit. However, Scripture interprets Scripture, and passages abound throughout Scripture that properly expand this commandment to include the whole range of sexual morals. (a) In Genesis 39:7–12 Joseph, an unmarried young man, refuses the request of Potiphar's wife to have sex with her. (b) In Matthew 5:28 Jesus condemns lustful looks as adultery committed in the heart. (c) Paul reminds us in 1 Corinthians 6:18–19 that sexual immorality is a sin against our own bodies, which are the temples of the Holy Spirit, who dwells in the hearts of Christians. (d) Paul, in Ephesians 5:3–4, forbids obscene or coarse talk.

Day 4 • Exodus 20:15–17

11. In Ephesians 4:28 Paul commands that thieves must stop their stealing—the very activity the command forbids. But Paul also adds a positive dimension, urging Christians to do useful work, which will enable us to "have something to share with those in need." Even the commandments stated in the negative have positive implications, as Paul points out here.

12. Once again the commandment speaks specifically to one issue: truth in testimony in court. But the more general concern of protecting others' personal reputation and good name should not be ruled out, as Exodus 23:1a shows, amplifying the commandment. Other passages also speak to this concern. (a) Psalm 15:1–5 includes speaking the truth, avoiding slander, and keeping oaths in behavior free from blame. (b) Proverbs 14:25 praises a truthful witness as one who saves lives.

13. This final principle contained in the last two commandments lies in the realm of the mind or heart. James compares the process that begins with coveting with the sexual desire that begins a human life. Just as sexual desire precedes the conception and birth of a human being who eventually dies, so coveting leads to sin that leads to death—that is, separation from God. This comparison helps us to see that, though coveting takes place in the mind, it is sin and brings about separation from God, just as other sins do.

Day 5 • Exodus 20:18–20

14. The Hebrew word for "trembled" is most descriptive: to sway or reel, even as the people "stayed at a distance" (v. 18). (a) God was impressing on the Israelites that He is a holy and all-powerful God. He wanted to strengthen their faith in Him so that they would not be inclined to sin against Him. (b) Both Moses and Jesus "stood between" God, in His righteous wrath over sin, and the people of God. Both spoke words of comfort to those terrified by God's holiness. But only Jesus could and did take on Himself the punishment for the sins of the world. The righteousness of Jesus stands between the holy God and our sin so that God does not see our sin but the righteousness of Jesus. (c) This righteous mediator continues to plead for us before the heavenly Father and will do so on the Last Day, when we face the judgment. This wonderful truth comforts and reassures us that our sins will not condemn us before God, since Jesus has already paid the penalty for our sins.

The Book of the Covenant

Exodus 20:21–23:33

Preparing for the Session

Central Focus

This session discusses the Book of the Covenant, a collection of the specific applications of the ten general "words" to the various dimensions of Israel's life.

Objectives

That the participant will be led to

1. repent of failure to keep the Law of God;
2. believe in the forgiveness of sins through the atoning sacrifice of Jesus Christ;
3. understand more clearly that God wills all of one's life to be in faith toward Him and fervent love toward one's neighbor;
4. willingly and gladly follow the instructions of God's will as one is empowered by the Spirit working through the Gospel.

For the Small-Group Leader

In contrast to the content of the first lesson, this lesson holds material far less known and of considerable difficulty in interpreting for our use today. In leading the discussion of your group, you will want to encourage comment and honest expression concerning the hard sayings of this section of Scripture. At the same time, you will want to be prepared to provide a biblically sound response.

The Book of the Covenant addresses fundamental issues faced by Israel as it applied the Ten Commandments to its way of life in the Promised Land. What were some of these issues? First, we find instructions regarding the purchase and treatment of servants or slaves (21:1–11). Here we can see how God directed His people in living in a God-pleasing way in this imperfect world (in their time and in ours today). Directions to treat servants or slaves kindly would have been unlikely in other cultures of the time.

Second, we find penalties laid down for wrongdoing. Group members may feel that some of the penalties prescribed for wrongdoing were unjustifiably harsh. Help your group members see the dangerous nature of the offenses (for example, abusing or cursing one's parents—Exodus 21:15, 17). What does the comparatively light penalties given such offenses today say about our own society? Help participants see the laws prescribing punishments that fit the crimes (for example, Exodus 21:23–25) as regulations establishing a just response and not as justification for retaliation. Offenses that would lead the Israelites into idolatry were regarded as extremely serious, since they would result in the subversion of God's plan to bring a Savior for the world through Israel as His chosen instrument.

Third, we find the command to rid the Promised Land of its idolatrous inhabitants. This was also a means of preserving Israel from lapsing into idolatry and unbelief and so shipwrecking God's plan to produce a Savior through Israel.

The overall emphasis of this lesson should be on how the Book of the Covenant applies the Ten Commandments within a social structure. These regulations were to govern Israel as God prepared His people to become His instrument in bringing the Messiah into the world for its salvation. They also remind us of the great distance we are from God and how necessary, therefore, are specific instructions to guide our relationships. Most pointedly the truth must come home to us that we are unable to keep such specific legalisms in all their details; there is no way that we can approach God by what we do. Only Jesus Christ can keep God's Law perfectly for us. Now we are free, through Him, to live not as we must but as the Spirit causes us to desire.

Small-Group Discussion Helps

Day 1 • Exodus 20:21–21:11

1. The commandment dealing with who is God and what is His authority over us must be first. It reminds us at the outset that what we do in response to God's commands is not our futile efforts to appease and

impress Him but is His due and our responsibility. He has made us and we are His (Psalm 100:3). Therefore, "You shall have no other gods before Me" (20:3). When we disregard in any way the other commandments, we are putting other gods before Him. We have made something or someone else, for the moment at least, first in our lives, rather than God. The First Commandment is always the first, precisely what Peter and John told the Sanhedrin (Acts 4:19).

2. People often mistakenly tend to think of worship as what we do as we come before God. (Check Micah 6:7.) Actually, God comes to us in our worship through the Gospel in Word and Sacraments. The tabernacle before which Israel later worshiped God was literally "a moving place" and is anticipated here by God's promise "to come to you and bless you." God's blessing is central to worship: in worship God offers to us and we receive His grace and mercy.

3. Significantly, after God gave His Law through Moses, He directed the building of an altar and a system of sacrifices. The people needed a way to pay for their sins. Since the fall into sin, no one can keep the commandments as God requires. The altar symbolized the presence of God, since through the sacrifices presented on the altar Israel received God's blessing and grace. So God's presence is among us in Word and Sacraments, means through which Christ's sacrifice for us is applied by faith to us.

4. The frequency of burnt offerings in Israel's worship and the fact that anyone could offer special offerings to express devotion to God should move us, His New Testament people, to be equally devoted to Him. Also, only the best was to be presented to God as a burnt offering. That reminds us to give of our best as we worship. The Hebrew name for burnt offering means "going up." Our worship and devotion is directed to God and is not to be measured by the satisfaction it gives us.

5. Certainly we need to be concerned that we keep our attention during worship focused on the Lord and on His Word and not on ourselves or on those who worship with us. We can make an effort to pay attention to what we are reading or singing and to listen to what is being said to us. We can consciously apply what we read and hear to us and not only to others. We can keep our eyes directed to the hymnbook and material we are using and to the chancel or pulpit and not on our neighbors. We can remember the meaning behind the symbols that are employed in the church furniture, the pastor's vestments, and other worship aids. The key to all of this is concentration and remembering what God has made us to be—His people in Christ.

6. (a) God did not command slavery, but He did permit it. Israelites were even permitted to have fellow Israelites as slaves, but for no longer than seven years, unless the slave voluntarily became a slave for life. Women slaves married by their masters were to be treated as wives who were not slaves. On the whole, servants or slaves were to be treated kindly, unlike the treatment of slaves in other cultures of that day. We might emphasize here how God's directions to us in our imperfect world make it more likely that we will do God's will on earth as it is in heaven (Matthew 6:10). A larger principle comes out of these stipulations regarding slaves that is definitely applicable to our day. Even misguided, if not totally wrong, social institutions (for example, communism) may be used by God through His people to improve the social order. (b) **Challenge question.** Slavery is not forbidden even in the New Testament. But Christian slave owners are commanded to treat their slaves with kindness and consideration, and Christian slaves are to serve their masters as serving the Lord Himself and in a way that commends faith in Christ. Christian slave owners are commanded to regard their Christian slaves as brothers and sisters in the Lord. It is no wonder that such evangelical pressures made slavery distasteful to Christians and eventually brought about the abolition of slavery.

Day 2 • Exodus 21:12–32

7. God's commands given to Israel through Moses provide for justice in this world. We need such justice to protect the innocent and the helpless in our sin-ridden world. However, God's own treatment of us goes beyond justice to mercy. Jesus satisfied God's justice when He paid the penalty for sin on the cross. God now extends mercy to us. Since we know that Jesus died also for those sins others commit against us, we can be like God and offer forgiveness and mercy to those who wrong us.

8. Christians continue to differ on the question of capital punishment. There is no question that capital punishment has been meted out inhumanely and unfairly in the

record of "man's inhumanity to man." However, the Bible clearly teaches that God allows governments to punish murderers by depriving them of their own lives. Going outside the law to deliberately kill a fellow human being shows contempt for God, who made the human being in His image and intends that people would walk in step with the Creator and live eternally with Him.

9. Kidnapping should be addressed in light of both of the commandments prohibiting killing and stealing. Kidnapping steals someone's supreme possession—the free use of life itself; only stealing life permanently through murder is a worse evil. This verse certainly puts in its proper light the present-day evil of terrorism with its toll of hostages. Kidnapping—even if its victims are called "hostages"—can never be justified.

10. Paul shows the fullness of the Law being kept through the new covenant in Jesus Christ, as he instructs children to obey their parents "for this pleases the Lord" (Colossians 3:20). Such obedience brings the old covenant promise to fruition "that it may go well with you and that you may enjoy long life on the earth" (Ephesians 6:3). In both instances Paul urges a positive reason for obeying the commandment. The motivation proceeds from faith in Christ and a desire to please the Lord.

Day 3 • Exodus 21:33–22:15

11. In daylight it is possible to assess more accurately how dangerous an assailant is. Darkness could justify defending oneself even by causing the attacker's death. This specific stipulation underscores that rather than kill or harm, even in self-defense, Christian love motivates to do as little harm as possible, even to one intent on evil. Self-protection is provided just as well by rendering an assailant helpless as by hurting or killing.

12. Restitution for crimes is commonly assessed in the courts of our land. When the person charged with making restitution does not have the resources to make restitution outright, the judge may require that restitution be made with future earnings. This form of penalty certainly provides a means of restoring some of the loss suffered by the victim and reinforces the notion that people are responsible for the harm they do to others. On the other hand, more severe penalties may provide a more effective deterrent to prevent similar crimes from being committed by others.

13. Sincere repentance will not attempt to get out of making restitution or to get by as lightly as possible but will desire to fully replace what was lost or destroyed. Sometimes this will not be possible, but where it is possible, the attempt will be made.

Day 4 • Exodus 22:16–23:9

14. The man who seduces the virgin must make matters right, either by paying the bride-price (paid by a bridegroom to compensate the bride's family for the loss of her help to the family) and marrying her, or, if the marriage is declined, paying the bride-price as a penalty. In either case, the man must make amends for seducing the woman.

15. **Challenge question.** Death might strike some participants as a harsh penalty for these sins. But consider that these sins are open revolt against God. The death penalty in these cases reflects the eternal death, or separation from God, that results from such revolt. Applying the death penalty in these cases would deter others from taking part in these sins. Furthermore, to allow these sins to go unchecked could result in the spiritual seduction of Israel, which would undermine God's plan to save the world from sin and death through the work of the Messiah, who would come through Israel.

16. Participants will undoubtedly think of many groups of people who need our help. Refugees from natural disasters and wars, residents of crime-ridden neighborhoods, the homeless in our own country, unborn children killed by abortions, children born to drug-addicted mothers—the list goes on and on. Be sure to communicate to class members that all of these are persons to whom Christ wants us to be a neighbor.

17. This question provides an opportunity to emphasize a proper understanding of Christian stewardship. All of our resources belong to the Lord; He has made us stewards, or trustees, of them. Some of our resources are to be used to share the Gospel with others through our congregation and church body. Whenever we use any of our resources without reference to God and His will for their use, we are holding back from the Lord and denying His claim to what is, in fact, His. In this sense, we are robbing God.

18. (a) This passage presents a stark contrast between the worship of God and the worship of the false gods and goddesses worshiped by other nations. The Lord's intention is to preserve human life, if possible, eternally. The Lord was willing to give the life of His own Son that ours might be preserved. In the Old Testament period firstborn sons were to be redeemed by the payment of an offering. The worship of Molech, however, demanded the sacrifice of infants and children. (b) The human sacrifice that the Lord seeks from us is our living for Him. Such a sacrifice not only honors God but benefits us beyond calculation!

19. (a) Remembering that they themselves had been foreigners in Egypt, the Israelites were to be particularly sensitive to the foreigners among them. This memory was to make them sympathetic to such people as they themselves had once been. (b) We are a nation of immigrants, just as the people of Israel were aliens. Remembering this would do much good in supporting new immigrants. We can assist such new neighbors in learning our language and customs, helping their children adjust to our schools, helping them find and keep employment, and in many other ways. Above all, we can welcome these new neighbors to our churches and help them find—or strengthen—a living relationship with Jesus, their Savior.

Day 5 • Exodus 23:10–33

20. God's directions concerning the Sabbath included rest for people, animals, and the soil. While the command to observe the Sabbath was tied to God's work in creating the universe—and so was a command to acknowledge, honor, and worship the Lord—the Sabbath provisions benefited the landless poor, laboring people, domestic animals, and even wildlife.

21. The Feast of Unleavened Bread was a weeklong observance immediately following Passover, during which the Israelites remembered the exodus from Egypt. During this period no yeast was to be eaten. The observance was also to include sacrifices. The Feast of Harvest (also called the Feast of Weeks or Pentecost) was celebrated seven weeks later, on the sixth day of the third month. It acknowledged God as the giver of the annual harvest by a sacrifice of a sheaf of grain, a lamb, and flour. None of the harvest was to be eaten until this sacrifice had been made. The Feast of Ingathering (also called the Feast of Tabernacles or Booths) was a week-long observance from the 15th through the 22d days of the seventh month. This third feast celebrated the completion of the harvest and reminded the Israelites that they had lived in temporary shelters—booths or tabernacles—after God brought them out of Egypt. Grain from the harvest, bread baked from flour from the harvest, and designated animals were to be offered to the Lord.

22. The angel was to guard Israel and guide the people to their destination. Some have suggested that this "angel" was an appearance by God Himself or may have been the Son of God before He appeared as the man Jesus.

23. (a) It is false tolerance to think of any idea—no matter the area of interest—on equal footing with the truth, as these common expressions imply. The Scriptures are our absolute point of reference as the truth. God commanded Israel not to live side by side with peoples who worshiped other gods, lest they mislead the Israelites into worshiping their false gods. Such a development would be disastrous for God's plan to save the world through the Messiah, who would come from Israel. (b) We also are to have nothing to do with false ideas, avoiding those who teach them. Instead, we are to occupy our minds with the truth that is taught in God's Word.

The Ratification of the Covenant

Exodus 24

Preparing for the Session

Central Focus

This session discusses the ratification of the covenant the Lord made with His people.

Objectives

That the participant will be led to

1. repent of sins, which make it impossible to stand before God on the basis of personal merit or worthiness;
2. grow in trust in the Lord Jesus Christ, who forgives us and shed His blood for all;
3. rejoice in the new covenant given through the shed blood of our Lord Jesus Christ;
4. appreciate more fully the wondrous gifts given in the Lord's Supper;
5. wholeheartedly say Amen to God's covenant with His people in Christ and gladly promise to lead a life worthy of his or her calling as one of God's people;
6. eagerly await the future coming of the Lord, when all will see Him face-to-face and believers will share in the messianic banquet.

For the Small-Group Leader

As you prepare to lead your discussion group this week, prepare carefully. Work through the study leaflet yourself first, without referring to the discussion helps in this leaders guide. Then go through the questions again, checking your responses with those suggested in this guide. If your answer does not agree with the comments in the leaders guide, look carefully at the question again.

Then read through the model lecture for this week's study. The lecture will also help to prepare you for the discussion. While you need not be concerned about covering in the group discussion matters that are not raised by the discussion questions themselves, the lecture will help you understand how the whole lesson fits together.

Some areas might be troublesome for some members of your group—God's punishment of Aaron's sons Nadab and Abihu, for instance. If you are uncertain about these matters yourself, you will want to do some additional study or check with your pastor or another Bible study leader whom you think might enlighten you.

Small-Group Discussion Helps

Day 1 • Exodus 24:1–2

1. As Hebrews 3:1–6 indicates, Moses in his faithful service testified to the future, the completion of God's plan of salvation in Jesus Christ. Thus, particular responsibilities and events in the life of Moses must be understood not solely in their historical context, but also as foreshadowing the mission of Christ for our salvation. Moses led the people of Israel out of bondage in Egypt through the Red Sea to the Promised Land. Jesus leads us out of our bondage to the devil, the world, and our flesh, on our way in our "heavenly calling" to its perfect fulfillment in heaven. We might emphasize also that Moses alone was called by God to serve as mediator between God and Israel, even as Jesus alone is our mediator between God and us.

2. We are sometimes called on to mediate between child and child, parent and/or spouse and child, friends, teacher and parent and/or child, at work, at home, in the congregation, at recreation. Mediation is very much a part of the expression of our Christian faith, centered in none other than Jesus Christ, who mediated for us before God. Matthew 5:14–16 is one of those scriptural jewels that truly deserves our memorization for constant reference. Reflecting the light that Jesus Christ brings to our world, nothing could be more our sacred duty than to reflect that light wherever we are and in whatever way we can.

3. Nadab and Abihu are among the Old Testament's tragic figures. Born to a position where they might have provided a great service to God, their disobedience instead brought them to destruction. (a) Because they acted contrary to God's command in a most unholy manner, they were consumed by a fire sent from the Lord. (b) They not only lost their place as priests before God, but their deaths reduced the number of Aaron's descendants.

4. Seventy descendants of Jacob, whose other name is Israel, settled in Egypt. That the people of Israel should select 70 elders to serve as advisors shows their identity to this patriarch. The 70 elders represented all of Israel.

5. The duties of the elders in Israel included (a) assisting Moses in governing the Israelites; (b) representing the nation in the installation of kings; and (c) representing the people in sacred assemblies. (The elders also assisted in judicial arbitration and in counseling and advising the Israelites in matters of faith.)

Day 2 • Exodus 24:3–8

6. (a) A little more than a month after declaring their willingness to abide by the covenant God had made with them, the Israelites broke their word by making and worshiping an idol. (b) Certainly in a public way we have made promises to God at Baptism (which most participants affirmed at confirmation) and at marriage. We make promises to God when installed as a teacher in a congregation's Christian education program and as an officer of the congregation or of an auxiliary organization. We also make private promises to God, for example, to pray or to attend worship more frequently. (c) *For personal reflection, not for sharing.* (d) God remains faithful to His promise to forgive and restore us for the sake of Jesus, our Savior, even though we have failed, and continue to fail miserably, to keep our promises to Him. We can depend on the Lord to be gracious to us.

7. Determining the human authorship of any book of the Bible is not of the greatest importance. What is important is our conviction that these human authors spoke by inspiration of God (2 Peter 1:20–21). Still, we look for evidence of human authorship, and no less an authority than Christ Himself ascribes authorship of the Pentateuch to Moses. Evidence within Exodus of Moses' authorship is found in Exodus 17:14; 24:4; 34:27.

8. (a) In Revelation 3:12, Jesus tells the first-century church of Philadelphia and all Christians threatened with persecution that "him who overcomes I will make a pillar in the temple of my God." (b) Galatians 2:9 is probably the source of our common expression "pillars of the church" as indication of importance and leadership, for Paul here names James (prominent in the Jerusalem congregation), Peter, and John "pillars." (c) 1 Peter 2:5 pictures the church and our place in it as "living stones," who offer "spiritual sacrifices acceptable to God through Jesus Christ." Peter's picture fits well with Paul's description of the church "built on the foundation of the apostles and prophets, with Christ Jesus Himself as the chief cornerstone." We make up the building, "no longer foreigners and aliens, but fellow citizens with God's people . . . to become a holy temple in the Lord" (Ephesians 2:19–21).

9. (a) Young Israelite men and Moses himself performed priestly duties at this point. Later only Aaron and his descendants were to perform these duties. (b) Opportunities for service in Christ's name within the congregation's worship, study, fellowship, and social ministries are widely available, though not necessarily every service is available to everyone. Also, we have many opportunities to serve the Lord in our own individual lives as we may love and serve others in the name of Jesus.

10. (a) Blood has been called the river of life and certainly is representative of life itself. The writer to the Hebrews argues that a will cannot be put into force unless the one who has made the will is dead; so the first covenant made by God to His people through Moses required the shedding of blood, resulting in the death of the sacrifice for sin. So the writer to the Hebrews concludes: "In fact, the law requires that nearly everything be cleansed with blood, and without the shedding of blood there is no forgiveness"(9:22). (b) The blood of the Old Testament sacrifices pointed ahead to the atoning sacrifice of Christ on the cross.

11. Jesus' words in the context of establishing the Lord's Supper echoes the words of Moses. In both cases, a covenant was being established through blood. In both cases the covenant established a fellowship between God and His people, whom He had redeemed. In both cases the covenant came into being through the services of a

mediator. The first covenant, established at Mount Sinai through Moses, looked forward to and was fulfilled by the second covenant established on Mount Calvary through Jesus. Participants may suggest other relationships.

Day 3 • Exodus 24:9–11

12. (a) In Exodus 33:20 God tells Moses that he could not see God (that is, in His full glory) and live, since Moses was a sinner, and sin cannot exist before God. However, to Moses, Hagar (Genesis 16:13), and others, including the Israelite elders, God revealed Himself in a way that shielded them from His full glory. (God told Moses that he might see God's "back.") In doing so, the Lord assured them that He was with them. In heaven, redeemed and purified from all sin, we shall see God's face (Revelation 22:4)—that is, we shall see Him in His full glory. (b) That God was being gracious to the Israelite elders in permitting them to see Him is indicated by the fact that "God did not raise His hand against" them.

13. (a) The elders ate and drank in the presence of God and in this way were in fellowship with Him. The disciples also ate and drank in the presence of God the Son and in this way were in fellowship with Him. The fellowship meal, in both cases, celebrated a covenant God had made with them—a covenant established with them as people God had redeemed. Both fellowship meals anticipated the arrival one day in a promised land. Participants may think of other ways in which the two meals are related. (b) Paul quotes Jesus in saying that the Lord's Supper is the "new covenant in My blood," which is to be observed in remembrance of Him (1 Corinthians 11:25). Paul says that whenever we observe the Lord's Supper, we are proclaiming His death, by which He established His gracious covenant with us, until He comes again at the end of time to take His church to live with Him in His glory in the eternal age to come.

Day 4 • Exodus 24:12–14

14. There can be no doubt about the origin or authority of laws and commands that God Himself inscribed with His own hand. The Ten Commandments express the eternal will of God for His people. Jesus came not to abolish this divinely given law but to fulfill it. It no longer accuses us before God.

15. (a) When Moses descended from Mount Sinai and discovered that the Israelites had already fallen into idolatry, he threw the stone tablets to the ground, and they broke into pieces. What a fitting way to express that the Israelites had broken the Law of God! (b) God then recalled Moses to the mountaintop and replaced the stone tablets with others. Israel preserved these tablets in the ark of the covenant, kept in the Most Holy Place of the tabernacle. They were eventually to be deposited in the inner sanctuary of the temple built by Solomon. We hear no more of them. No doubt they were lost or destroyed when the temple was sacked and demolished by the Babylonians. But though the stone tablets themselves were lost, the commands of God were enshrined and preserved in the Bible and in the hearts of God's people.

16. (a) Aaron and Hur failed abysmally when they were unable to prevent the Israelites from falling into the sin of idolatry. Even worse, they directed and assisted in the making of the idol the Israelites worshiped! (b) Naming situations where we take someone's place in advising, supporting, and guiding others should quicken our awareness of the tragedy of failing to do this well, even as Aaron failed Moses and gave in to the people of Israel's demand to make a golden calf as an idol (Exodus 32). Teachers (who act in the place of parents and the community as a whole) carry a heavy responsibility here, as do parents themselves, who represent God to their children (Ephesians 6:4; Colossians 3:20–21). Coaches, employers, civil servants, and anyone who represents authority over someone else has this responsibility. Knowing God's will and seeking His power and strength are important in fulfilling these responsibilities. How comforting, as well, to know that forgiveness is available when we fail to carry out our responsibilities as we should!

Day 5 • Exodus 24:15–18

17. The pillar of cloud and fire that led the Israelites after the exodus from Egypt was a manifestation of the glory of the Lord. It assured God's people of His presence.

18. **Challenge question.** The 40 days and nights in Christ's life are associated with the period of His temptation by Satan in the wilderness. Christ's withdrawal in solitude took place at the beginning of His ministry for

His strengthening. It climaxed with His overcoming temptation that covered the gamut of human desire, which Satan would use to separate Jesus from His Father's purpose. Christ endured this temptation in the wilderness as our forerunner, so that we could endure and with His strength let nothing get between us and Him. Moses listened to God on the mountain; Jesus heard and communed with God His Father as He spoke God's Word to defeat Satan. The two accounts underscore basic truths: the Law proclaimed on Sinai condemns us; Christ came to keep that Law perfectly for us. Moses represented and interceded for the people. Jesus, in a much fuller sense, represented us as He did battle with the devil.

19. We are thinking here of far more than the prayer corner or worship time or table prayer—as important as these times of retreat and reflection are. Remembering that Moses the busy leader disappears for a considerable time to hear God speak to him, and he talks with God within the framework of his responsibilities, do we look for this privilege to communicate with God within the scope of our responsibilities? Anyone in any vocation may experience the thrill of conversation with God while performing a job well, a vocation of service for others.

The Tabernacle and Its Furnishings

Exodus 25–27

Preparing for the Session

Central Focus

This session discusses the tabernacle and its furnishings. The lesson will focus particularly on the significance of the furniture.

Objectives

That the participant will be led to

1. repent of sin against God;
2. believe in the forgiveness achieved by the atoning sacrifice of Jesus Christ;
3. frequently go to the means of grace to receive this forgiveness from the Lord;
4. rejoice in the tabernacling presence of God in Christ among His people;
5. appreciate more fully that the Lord delivered the church in order to dwell in her midst and evoke her worship.

For the Small-Group Leader

At first glance, there really seems to be little that is truly spiritually strengthening or uplifting in details pertaining to the construction of the ark, table, lampstand, tabernacle, altar of burnt offering, courtyard, and the preparation of oil for the lampstand. But devoted study of these three chapters will give far more understanding of and appreciation for the place of the tabernacle and its furnishings in God's plan of salvation, all foreshadowing God's amazing grace for us.

Here is a suggestion: Perhaps you can find someone who has a gift for making scale models and who will model the tabernacle and its furnishings. A model would certainly help to visualize this structure, which is described in such detail in this lesson. Displaying such a scale model somewhere within your church building would also be a great way to help publicize LifeLight Bible study. It might even stimulate the beginning of a permanent collection of models for the use of Bible class and Sunday school teachers in your congregation!

Small-Group Discussion Helps

Day 1 • Exodus 25:1–9

1. (a) The offerings are to be received "for Me [God] from each man whose heart prompts him to give" (v. 2). The ancient peoples, including the Jews, saw the heart, rather than the mind, as the center of motivation. We still reflect that influence when we ask, "Where's your heart?" or describe someone as "coldhearted." A key verse presenting stewardship in its noblest expression is one in which Paul shows his indebtedness to the verse before us, as he writes the Corinthians: "Each man should give what he has decided in his heart to give, not reluctantly or under compulsion, for God loves a cheerful giver" (2 Corinthians 9:7). (b) 2 Corinthians 8:1–15 and 9:6–15 are important passages on Christian giving. Some of the principles Paul states in these passages are (1) Christian giving must begin with the giving of ourselves to the Lord (8:5); (2) giving is a "grace"—that is, it results from the work of the Holy Spirit within us (8:7); (3) Christian giving is a response to the complete self-sacrifice of Jesus Christ (8:9); (4) Christians give according to their means—it is the willingness to give, not the amount given, that makes Christian giving acceptable to God (8:12; 9:7); (5) Christian giving provides for the needs of others out of our own plenty (8:13–14); (6) God rewards generosity with greater blessings (9:6); (7) Christian giving results from a trust that God will provide for our own needs (9:10); (8) Christian giving causes thanksgiving and praise to be given to God (9:11–14); (9) Christian giving is the product of thankfulness to God (9:15).

2. **Challenge question.** What the Israelites were to offer for the tabernacle and its furnishings are listed in verses 3–7. Each of the items is beautiful and set apart from the mundane, as if to remind the Israelites that we are to worship God "in the splendor of His holiness" (Psalm 96:9).

3. (a) Most, if not all, of this supply must have come from the large presents of gold and silver the Egyptians gave Israel before the Exodus. Now we know why God commanded the Israelites to ask for these gifts from the Egyptians and why God disposed the Egyptians to give such valuable gifts to the Israelites. (b) We obtain the gifts we give to God from many sources, but especially from what has been given to us and from what we have earned. Whatever the source of our income or wealth, we recognize that it all comes from the bountiful hand of God, who entrusts us with it that we may use it in a way that honors and acknowledges Him.

4. (a) Stephen's overview of Israel's history as he witnessed to his faith in Jesus Christ included reference to the tabernacle as "a dwelling place for the God of Jacob," although it was Solomon who constructed the permanent edifice. But Stephen, quoting Isaiah, reminds his listeners that "the Most High does not live in houses made by men," for "Heaven is My throne, and the earth is My footstool" (Acts 7:48–49). (b) It is our human need that requires the visible structure to remind us of the immanence and transcendency of God, who is always dwelling with us. We need to set aside a place as well as time for worship.

Day 2 • Exodus 25:10–22

5. Both references describe the ark as the place where God is enthroned between the cherubim (winged figures). 2 Kings 19:15 and Psalm 99:1 also describe the cherubim as marking the place of God's throne. Later, the ark's presence in Jerusalem would designate it as God's earthly royal city (Psalm 9:11). So the ark, and particularly the cherubim on the cover, symbolized for the Israelites God's enthronement in their midst, even as the tabernacle assured them of God's dwelling with them. We need, and employ, similar reminders of His presence with us in the structure and furnishing of our church buildings and in the artifacts of our homes.

6. Humanity has always recognized the preciousness of gold. Wood, on the other hand, is usually common and relatively cheap. The Lord can and does use what the world regards as precious and what the world regards as common. This applies to people too. In fact, the most common and ordinary of people can be the very people God chooses for extraordinary places in His kingdom.

7. (a) With our inclination to place God here or there, we must underscore His presence with us wherever we are, as the ark's poles did for Israel. We should want to feel and experience, as David did (Psalm 139), God's closeness no matter where we are. (b) Encourage participants to say how the awareness that God is with them, wherever they are, is comforting and encouraging to them in their own lives.

Day 3 • Exodus 25:23–40

8. The table was to provide a place for the "bread of the Presence," or showbread. The table itself is seldom mentioned in Scripture, even when the bread of the Presence itself is referred to, as, for example, in 1 Samuel 21:6.

9. The 12 loaves, one for each tribe, served as a perpetual memorial to God. Thus the tribes consecrated all of their labor and the fruits of their hands to God, acclaiming all to be God's blessings. The bread of the Presence also provided nourishment for the priests. God nourishes His people (increases their faith) (a) through His written Word, (b) through Jesus, the incarnate Word and bread of life, and (c) through Holy Communion.

10. As with the bread of the Presence, the lampstand (besides its practical function of providing light) became a symbol too. (a) God Himself was symbolized by its light, (b) as was the coming Savior, Jesus. (c) In John's vision the seven lampstands represented the seven churches to which God had a special message to speak through John. Christ was standing among the lampstands, that is, among the churches.

11. The lighted candles on the altars of our churches may represent different truths to different people, but generally the lighted candles are meant to represent the presence of Christ among us as we worship.

Day 4 • Exodus 26

12. (a) The sin of the Israelites separated them from the holy God, as Isaiah declares. This, in fact, is true of all people, including us. But Jesus has made atonement for our sin and has covered us with His holiness, ending the separation between God and His people. (b) Only priests were allowed to come into the first room, the Holy Place, which they did regularly (daily). And only the High

Priest, and he but once a year, on the Day of Atonement, might enter the second room, the Most Holy Place. This indicated that sin continued to separate people from God and that an atonement for sin was still needed—the atonement that would be made by Jesus, the Messiah.

13. (a) The typical plan of many churches shows an origin in the tabernacle plan. The threefold division of chancel, nave, and narthex correspond to the Most Holy Place, the Holy Place, and courtyard of the tabernacle. The eternal lamp, candelabra, and candlesticks obviously show their relationship with the lampstand and its lamps of the Holy Place. The table finds representation in the chancel altar, which also takes the place of the altar of sacrifice in the courtyard. For on the altar of the cross Christ "once for all" sacrificed Himself for the sins of the people (Hebrews 7:26–27). (b) When Jesus died on the cross to atone for our sins, the curtain separating the Holy Place from the Most Holy Place was torn in two pieces, showing that our sins had now been removed and that we are made holy in Jesus. Nothing now prevents us from entering into the very presence of God—now in prayer and in person when we are in heaven. (c) The open chancel rail, found in most Protestant churches, depicts the tearing of the curtain in the temple as Christ, through His mediatorship, opens the way for us to approach God (Hebrews 10:19–25).

14. (a) Paul tells us that all barriers have been removed—not only the barrier of sin that kept us from God but also those barriers between Jews and Gentiles and between men and women, so far as membership in God's kingdom and as His people are concerned. We all have equal access to God through faith in Christ, our Savior. (b) You should have no difficulty in naming the walls that divide people socially, economically, culturally, racially, religiously, politically, nationally. What is important is that we are able to see that our only hope to demolish these walls is in Jesus Christ, who truly makes us one (Galatians 3:28). If that is our genuine hope, then our mission work and witnessing, personally and through others, is something we must do if we want God's will to be done on earth among us and His kingdom to come among us. By now, it is hoped, you will be comfortable enough to talk to your small-group members about some of the dividing walls in your life, as you express also your firm conviction that in Jesus Christ they can be torn down.

Day 5 • Exodus 27

15. The tabernacle/temple and its sacrifices are no longer needed, since Christ has come to offer atonement for all sins once and for all. The old covenant, with its system of sacrifices, was temporary—to be in force only until Christ should come. Now that He has come and has made the perfect and complete atonement that only He could make, the old covenant—together with its tabernacle/temple and system of worship—has been set aside forever.

16. While we build, consecrate, and use buildings where we gather to worship God and to receive His grace through the Gospel, God has given no directions as to how these structures are to be built or arranged, the furnishings with which they are equipped, or the exact way in which we are to structure or order our worship. Nevertheless, the New Testament does refer to temples. (a) The New Testament temple on this earth is the body of Jesus, for in Jesus, God the Holy Trinity was to be found on this earth. (b) Each individual Christian is called a temple, for God the Holy Spirit dwells and works within each Christian. (c) The church as a whole is God's temple, for God remains with it and works within it. Each Christian is a part of this temple of God on earth. From these references we can see that God now dwells on this earth within *people* not *structures.*

The Priesthood

Exodus 28–29

Preparing for the Session

Central Focus

This session discusses the Old Testament priesthood—its garments, ordination, and roles—and shows how it relates to Christ, the ministers of the Gospel, and the priesthood of all believers.

Objectives

That the participant will be led to

1. repent of sins, which make it impossible to stand before the holy God without a mediator;
2. believe in the Lord Jesus Christ, who is the High Priest and atoning sacrifice for all;
3. receive by faith the forgiveness and holiness that Christ bestows through the ministers of the Gospel;
4. appreciate more fully his or her role as a priest of God in Christ;
5. eagerly await the Last Day, when believers will be made perfect and whole and will enter the heavenly sanctuary to be with the Lord forever.

For the Small-Group Leader

God's promise that His Word brings results holds true also for our chapters under consideration this week. Careful study uncovers important truths that not only contribute to our knowledge of Israel's priesthood but are most applicable to everyday life today.

At a time when there may be somewhat less appreciation for the clergy, you can use this lesson to guide class members to think through and talk about the promise and responsibility of ministry today. Some group members may want to speak about the shortcomings of ministers they have known. Suggest that it would be more beneficial to the group to concentrate, instead, on what God has to say about the ministry in His Word. Where individual ministers fall short, we may pray for them and, where appropriate, encourage and counsel with them personally.

Small-Group Discussion Helps

Day 1 • Exodus 28:1–14

1. (a) Verse 2 states the reason clearly for priestly garments: "to give him [Aaron, the high priest] dignity and honor." (b) Individuals may certainly have different reactions to, and see less or more in the use of, clergy vestments, but the two words here describing why priestly garments should be made and worn are reasons, still today, for the use of vestments. For dignity: the vestment plays down size and physique and makes the pastor less likely to veil God's glory in our corporate worship. For honor: the focus of our worship, rather than resting on the pastor, is rightly directed to God, and the pastor is revered only to the degree that he has been commissioned by the congregation to lead in that worship. Without vestments, it would be only too easy for individual worshipers to dwell on the pastor's appearance, making him a distraction to worship. With vestments, the pastor's appearance may underscore the glory of God and how beautiful it is to worship Him.

2. (a) Deuteronomy 31:9–13 directs the priests, who carried the ark of the covenant from place to place during the journey to the Promised Land, to read the law of Moses to the people and to remind them of their covenant obligations. (b) Hebrews 5:1–2 states that priests served God as they offered sacrifice for sins and dealt gently with those who were ignorant or going astray. (c) If we view the pastor as Christ's under-shepherd, who proclaims through the Gospel Christ's sacrifice of Himself for our sins and calls the individual to confession of sin by means of the Law so that Christ's atonement is genuinely and gratefully accepted, we should see the priestly duties of service before God as very similar to those of pastors today.

3. (a) An ongoing priesthood would be needed when Moses died. Israel would need the priesthood until Jesus would come to make the once-and-for-all atonement to which the Old Testament sacrifices looked for-

ward. (b) Paul instructs Titus to appoint men as pastors who are without serious faults. They are to be faithful husbands and effective parents, humble, patient, temperate, gentle, honest, hospitable, principled, and self-disciplined. (c) Participants will probably choose various qualities they regard as most important in a pastor, but probably close to the top of the list will be such qualities as a sincere and mature faith, faithfulness to the Gospel and Scripture, an ability to relate well to people, and skill as a preacher and teacher.

Day 2 • Exodus 28:15–30

4. (a) Precious stones adorned both of these pieces of Aaron's vestments. In both cases the stones represented the tribes of Israel: Aaron "will bear the names of the sons of Israel over his heart on the breastpiece of decision as a continuing memorial before the LORD" (v. 29). (b) Not only did these stones serve as memorials before the Lord, but they surely also reminded the high priest of his duty to pray for the Israelites and to remember their spiritual needs.

5. The Urim and Thummim were used by the priest to determine God's will in matters to be decided. Thus, the Urim and Thummim could have been shaped stones used as dice for the "casting of lots" to get God's direction, as in 1 Samuel 28:6.

6. Christians today also have God-given resources to draw on when making decisions. These include (a) Scripture, (b) prayer, and (c) the counsel of Christian leaders or friends.

Day 3 • Exodus 28:31–43

7. (a) While Jesus was referring to grapevines rather than pomegranates, a similar application might be made to any fruit. Christians, by remaining connected to Jesus through faith, are to bear the fruit of faith—worship and praise of God and works of love and service to others in the name of Jesus. (b) A Jewish tradition was that a rope tied to the priest's ankle—the other end outside the tabernacle—could be pulled "gently" to determine whether he was still alive in case the bells on the robe stopped tinkling! But other Hebrew traditions suggest better reasons for the bells: they typified the proclamation and expounding of the Law by the high priest; they were a musical offering of praise; they marked kingly dignity; and they were a call to vigilance and attention to priestly duties. The last agrees best with the statement of verse 35: "so that he will not die." The worshipers, who waited outside the tabernacle while the high priest ministered inside, could hear the bells tinkling and knew that the high priest was ministering on their behalf before God.

8. (a) God denounces prophets, or pastors, who "prophesy [or preach] out of their own imagination" and don't proclaim God's Word. (b) The priest, or pastor, "is the messenger of the LORD Almighty," who must not by his teaching cause people to stumble. (c) The pastor's ministry is built on Jesus Christ, and it is God who prospers that ministry. Pastors are not to place anything on that foundation that does not honor or glorify Christ. (d) The pastor is to endure "like a good soldier of Christ Jesus." All is to be endured "for the sake of the elect, that they too may obtain the salvation that is in Christ Jesus." (e) Those leaders who teach the faith will be "judged more strictly." (f) We may help and encourage pastors to fulfill the responsibilities of their ministry by praying for them; hearing faithfully and heeding the Word of God they proclaim and teach; responding to calls for service in God's kingdom as we have the time, talents, and resources to do so; offering words of encouragement and gratitude; and in other ways that participants may suggest.

Day 4 • Exodus 29:1–21

9. (a) Moses washed the high priest and priests for their cleansing. Christians are washed of their sins by Holy Baptism. (b) Second, the high priest and priests were vested. Christians are to clothe themselves with the righteousness of Jesus by trusting in Him as their Savior. (c) Third, Aaron as high priest and his sons as priests were anointed with oil. Christians are anointed with the Holy Spirit, who gives and strengthens faith.

10. (a) As God called Aaron to be Israel's high priest, so He called Jesus, His Son, to be our High Priest. (b) Aaron was anointed. So, too, the Spirit of the Lord anointed Christ. (c) Aaron was one of many mediators in the long line of the priesthood; Jesus Christ is our one mediator between God and us, because He gave Himself as a ransom for all.

Day 5 • Exodus 29:22–46

11. (a) Some parts of some of the offerings were to go to the priests as part of their living. The priests and Levites were also later to receive land throughout Israel, the produce of which was to provide a living for those who served in the tabernacle or temple, and the tithes given by all the Israelites was devoted to the maintenance of the temple and its ministry. (b) The offerings we give to the Lord as one expression of our worship are used for a number of practical purposes to advance the Lord's kingdom by the proclamation of the Gospel. One of these practical uses is to provide a living for pastors and other ministers who serve full-time in the ministry of the Gospel.

12. Daily worship provides us a constant source of strength: opportunity for prayer, requests, and thanksgiving to God; time to express and release concerns with the certainty of being heard; regularity that encourages a thankful heart; and the feeling gained that there is nothing, absolutely nothing, more beautiful, pleasant, invigorating, and encouraging than to enter into God's presence. (a) Psalm 55:17 presents the testimony of David, who brought his cries for help to the Lord repeatedly. (b) Daniel 6:10 tells us how Daniel followed the traditional Jewish practice of offering prayers to God three times a day. This Old Testament example encourages us to devote a portion of each day to prayer and worship. (c) Jesus, in the Lord's Prayer, teaches us to pray for the necessities of life needed "today"—implying that we pray each day.

13. This question requires a personal and honest answer. Hopefully, our study this week has helped us to appreciate the beauty and good of worship forms, always seen as avenues of approach to God through Jesus Christ, our High Priest.

The Elements of Worship

Exodus 30–31

Preparing for the Session

Central Focus

This session deals with the tabernacle's incense altar and bronze basin and with the ransom money, the workers' God-given skill, and the Sabbath. It will concentrate on the tabernacle's significance for the church's liturgical worship.

Objectives

That the participant will be led to

1. repent of sins against God;
2. believe in the forgiveness of sins that comes from Christ, who paid the ransom price in his or her place;
3. rejoice in the washing of regeneration received in Baptism;
4. attend church to receive the means of grace;
5. appreciate more fully the church's historic liturgy;
6. thank God for the skills and abilities He has given so he or she might serve Him.

For the Small-Group Leader

This lesson, too, focuses on chapters in sacred Scripture that most of us tend to skip over or read cursorily. But with careful reading and study, a little imagination, and a desire to apply God's Word to today's concerns, we experience once again the truth of the great statement in the letter to the Hebrews regarding the Word of God: "For the Word of God is living and active. Sharper than any double-edged sword, it penetrates even to dividing soul and spirit, joints and marrow; it judges the thoughts and attitudes of the heart. Nothing in all creation is hidden from God's sight. Everything is uncovered and laid bare before the eyes of Him to whom we must give account" (Hebrews 4:12–14).

Small-Group Discussion Helps

Day 1 • Exodus 30:1–10

1. Blood from the sacrificed animal was to be applied to the horns of the incense altar once a year, on the Day of Atonement, by the high priest before he entered into the Most Holy Place. This was to make atonement for all of the sins of the Israelites during the previous year.

2. (a) The burning incense, as its smoke filled the room and drifted into the Most Holy Place beyond the curtain, represented the prayers and devotion of God's people. (b) Our prayers are taken into the presence of God by the Holy Spirit, who expresses our imperfect and stumbling prayers in just the way they ought to be put before God and in accordance with His holy will, and by Jesus Himself, whose sacrifice on the cross sanctifies our prayers and makes them acceptable to God.

3. As the people prayed outside the temple, the priest Zechariah burned the incense to represent their prayers as they came before God. In the revelation given to John, an angel brings a burning bowl of incense into the presence of God to represent the prayers of God's people. The prayers of God's people are commonly symbolized in Scripture by the fragrant smoke of incense, as these Bible verses indicate. These passages assure us that our prayers do come before God, that they are pleasing to Him, and that He accepts them as worship. The second stanza of this week's hymn underscores how daily our "endless prayer" rises in the name of Jesus, making it "like sweet perfume." We are able to penetrate the veil that separates us from God only through Jesus Christ, who has gained access for us.

4. More precious than gold are (a) wisdom (that is, insight into the will of God revealed to us in the Gospel), (b) faith in Jesus Christ as our Savior, and (c) the precious blood of Christ, by which we are redeemed and cleansed from sin. The gold that overlaid the altar of incense represented these precious spiritual realities.

5. (a) **Challenge question.** The Leviticus passage describes how the priest carried a censer of coals from

the altar of burnt offering in the courtyard to the altar of incense (implied), the coals used to burn the incense. The smoke prevented the priest from seeing the cover of the ark of the covenant, where God had placed His presence. On the annual Day of Atonement, when the high priest entered the inner room, the Most Holy Place, the officiating priest was screened by the smoke of the incense and was preserved from death when he, a sinner, should come into the presence of the holy God. (b) Our prayers, like incense, rise up before God. Jesus' sacrifice of Himself shields us from God's punishment of sin.

Day 2 • Exodus 30:11–21

6 (a) This is a pointed reminder of the equal value of souls; thus the ransom money is the same for rich and poor alike. (b) Jesus gave *Himself* as a ransom for all.

7. The tabernacle was that place where God chose to meet with His people and to speak with them.

8. (a) The women of Israel offered their bronze mirrors to make the basin for washing. These mirrors were probably prized possessions of these women. (b) We rightly consider our stewardship of self and things to be acts of worship too.

9. (a) We are ready and able to worship when we are cleansed from sin by the redeeming work of Christ, applied to us through the Gospel, which is also extended to us through Holy Baptism. We receive this redemption by faith. (b) Encourage group members to speak about how they put themselves in a suitable frame of mind for worship. For example: We make sure we get up in plenty of time on Sunday morning so no one has to be rushed getting ready for church. We make sure we have picked out the night before what we are going to wear. That way no one feels harried or upset but can be relaxed and in a good frame of mind when we get to Sunday school and church.

Day 3 • Exodus 30:22–38

10. (a) **Challenge question.** Note that the same threat is repeated in 31:14. There it is a punishment for desecrating the Sabbath, while here the punishment is for the secular use of the anointing oil and incense. That helps us to find our answer. The oil, incense, and keeping of the Sabbath are all signs of the covenant between God and His people. The seriousness of obligations assumed by God's people and the dreadful consequences of forgetting those obligations are underscored by the threat of execution or banishment. (b) The sin that cuts us off from God is the sin of unbelief. Those who have never believed have never been in God's kingdom. Those who believe but then fall into unbelief are cut off from God as a result. We ought to regard this prospect seriously and take care to nourish and guard our faith.

11. (a) As Prophet, Jesus spoke God's Word by preaching and teaching people, both in groups and individually. Jesus continues His prophetic work today through the preaching and teaching of the church. "He who listens to you listens to Me" (Luke 10:16). (b) As Priest, Jesus sacrificed Himself on the cross to atone for the sins of all. As our Priest, Jesus also intercedes for us today. (c) As King, Jesus rules over all. He rules over the church on earth by His gracious Word, and He rules over the church in heaven by His glory.

12. Participants will probably come up with a long list of things we dedicate and so set apart for use in our worship, especially churches and their furnishings, Communion and baptismal vessels, and such.

Day 4 • Exodus 31:1–11

13. The Lord, through His Spirit, had given Bezalel, Oholiab, and the craftsmen who worked under their supervision the skills and inspiration needed to fashion beautiful materials and furnishings for the tabernacle.

14. (a) Encourage group members to speak of specific tasks God has given them as parent, Sunday school teacher, church member, homemaker, provider, care giver, worker in some vocation, neighbor, friend, contributor. (b) For each task God has given us, He has also given us the needed equipment: patience, love, various skills, personal attributes, talents, time, strength, intelligence, concern, and such.

15. Christians particularly, who feel accountable to God, will recognize the importance of recognizing what God has called them to do and to use the skills and abilities He has given them as tools with which to accomplish those tasks He has given. Christians know they are servants and stewards.

Day 5 • Exodus 31:12–18

16. Observing the Sabbath as a day of rest; regular, daily prayers; offering prescribed sacrifices; circumcision; observing dietary laws; and other practices marked the Israelites as different from their Gentile neighbors. Christians also will practice a lifestyle that sets them apart from unbelieving neighbors—worship, prayer, stewardship that supports the Lord's work, and godly behavior are some of these external signs of living in a covenant with God. A constructive attitude; speaking the truth in love; humility that proclaims thanks for God's forgiveness—these are also signs of one who lives as a person redeemed by Christ.

17. The Sabbath was (a) to remind the Israelites that God had made them holy (set apart) to Him; (b) and it was a sign of the covenant between God and Israel. Israelites who refused to observe the Sabbath were refusing to live in a covenant with God. Such a person was rejecting the God of Israel—the worst of all sins. Such a person was to be cut off from Israel (and was to be deprived of life itself), since this person had rejected God.

18. (a) The Sabbath and other ceremonial laws have served this purpose of preparing Israel for the coming of the Messiah. (b) God our Creator knows the limitations of our humanity (particularly after the weakening brought about by sin). He knows that regular physical rest is a requirement for a healthy body and mind. Furthermore, and more important, the Sabbath directed Israel's attention to their God. The day of rest permitted, and encouraged, a contemplation of the Lord and of the blessings He had shown to Israel, particularly the blessing of redemption from bondage in Egypt and the coming redemption from sin through the Messiah. While we are no longer bound to the compulsory inactivity imposed by the Sabbath under the Old Covenant, we do well to leave time for rest and refreshment, both physical and spiritual. (c) Already in the time of the apostles Christians began to worship on the first day of the week, Sunday, to commemorate the Lord's resurrection from the dead. In this sense Easter comes every week!

The Rupture of the Covenant

Exodus 32–33

Preparing for the Session

Central Focus

This session discusses how Israel broke the covenant and how Moses interceded. From these chapters we will learn more of Christ's role as intercessor and of the nature of Christian prayer in Christ's name.

Objectives

That the participant will be led to

1. repent of the old Adam's inclinations, which go against God and set up idols;
2. believe in the Lord Jesus Christ, who atoned for sin and intercedes for His people;
3. rejoice in the Lord's continual and gracious presence with His people on the journey to the Promised Land;
4. intend to amend his or her sinful life by the power of the Holy Spirit working through the Gospel.

For the Small-Group Leader

A major purpose of LifeLight is to lead people to see how totally practical and wholly applicable the Scriptures are to daily life. Through personal and daily Bible study, LifeLight participants will discover the satisfaction of searching the Scriptures.

This lesson brings this point home. Up to now we have been caught in many details that describe how God gave His covenant to the Israelites and the many stipulations applying that covenant. We have also read detailed instructions regarding worship and rituals. But now we see the unevenness of the human response, the inequities of human doings, how people step over the line between right and wrong and miss the mark of God's requirements. In other words, people sin. Sin looms large at the foot of the mountain of God as the Israelites dance before the golden calf and proclaim it the god who led them out of Egypt. And all this happens as Moses meets on the mountaintop with the God of their fathers Abraham, Isaac, and Jacob.

How is it possible for human beings to fall so far short of God's covenant at the very moment when the goodness and glory of God is overwhelmingly evident in their lives? But, in fact, their behavior is typical of our own human experience and situation. So this lesson's discussion might turn a bit more introspective. Gently encourage the members of your discussion group to turn the spotlight on themselves. Out of this self-examination will flow the plea in which we may join together: "God have mercy on me, a sinner" (Luke 18:13).

Small-Group Discussion Helps

Day 1 • Exodus 32:1–10

1. (a) When things don't seem to be going well, no matter how that may be measured, (b) isn't loveless criticism really a display of impatience with God? After all, the source of Israel's impatience that led them to want a golden calf as a god seemed to rest on the fact that Moses was staying too long on the mountain. But God saw this impatience with their leader, leading them to apostasy, as a violation of His covenant with the people. Similarly, we might examine our feelings to see if what we hold against someone else fundamentally springs from an impatience with God Himself. John observes: "For anyone who does not love his brother, whom he has seen, cannot love God, whom he has not seen" (1 John 4:20).

2. Aaron's compliance with the people's request to "make us gods" suggests a caving in to this fundamentally wrong request. We probably find it easy to condemn Aaron. As the high priest and brother of Moses, he surely forgot or minimized his responsibility to the people, to say nothing about personal character weakness. But let's not stop with a denunciation of Aaron; we must see how easily we forget our responsibilities to one another in our service and functions or minimize the proper influence we have on one another.

3. **Challenge question.** We see the full reality of what Israel was doing when we compare their actions before the golden calf to the ceremony in which they had earlier ratified God's covenant with them. In both cases, the Israelites presented fellowship offerings and then took part in a ceremonial meal. They were making a covenant with the golden calf as they had earlier made a covenant with God. In others words, they were replacing the Lord with the calf idol! This idol had now become their lord.

4. (a) One thing leads to another, we are inclined to say, and that is true of the process of sin in our lives. If we can convince ourselves that God is not so important to us after all, or rationalize that He doesn't care what we do, or think He will appreciate our decisions to do what we want to do, then one sin leads to another. In the case of the people of Israel, their idolatry led them "to indulge in revelry." The Hebrew suggests sexual connotations in the activity. We should note, too, that when we do not allow God to be what God should be in our lives, anything can happen. The common social ills of our society are best addressed by sharpening consciences to see God's rightful place of authority over every individual's life. (b) Answers will vary. We need to be on our guard against a lackadaisical attitude on the one hand and a lack of trust in the Holy Spirit's presence and power on the other.

5. Israel was God's people so long as they remained in the covenant relationship the Lord had established with them at Sinai. In practicing idolatry, the Israelites had renounced that covenant relationship and so were no longer God's people. They had renounced their ties with Him. Now they were related to Moses only by blood.

Day 2 • Exodus 32:11–14

6. Moses based his plea for the people on God's own words: he underscored God's special relationship to Israel; he reminded God how intimately God was associated with Israel by other nations and thus must protect His name as expressed in Israel's future; he pointed back to God's promises made to Abraham, Isaac, and Jacob, to be fulfilled in their descendants for the welfare of all nations.

7. (a) Both passages present us with remarkable instances of men of God who boldly attempt to prevail upon God to change His mind. Both intercede for sinners. However, there are important differences. Abraham intercedes for a people with whom God had not established a covenant, whereas Moses intercedes for a people whom God had claimed as His own. Abraham appealed to God's justice and fairness; Moses appealed to God's Word of promise. Abraham's intercession fails to save Sodom and Gomorrah, since those cities did not contain even the minimal number of righteous people Abraham dared to suggest, although God Himself delivered Lot, his wife, and daughters before destroying the cities. Moses succeeded in persuading God to spare the Israelites as His covenant people, although those who instigated the idolatry and totally abandoned the Lord were punished with death. Participants may suggest other similarities and differences. (b) Moses had great faith in God's mercy and grace and believed that God would stand by the promises He had made in regard to Israel. His is the confidence that clings to faith in God's grace. (c) At the same time, the passage shows us that God binds Himself to His Word and promises and wishes to yield to prayers that are based on them. God is a God of mercy and grace.

Day 3 • Exodus 32:15–30

8. Both the Scriptures and our experience testify that there is an anger that, when vented, brings healing, even as there is an anger that, when allowed to smolder within, only brings damage to self and to others. It is a mistaken caricature of the Christian life that outspoken and hard-hitting words and feelings must be suppressed. They, too, can be spoken in love and may be necessary because of the circumstance.

9. Aaron's excuses are classic examples of excuse-making. The blame is put on someone else. Or, "it" just happened, the result of circumstances, luck, fate, destiny, genes, whatever. Just as Aaron attempted to shift the blame to the Israelites or to events he could not control, so both Adam and Eve attempted to shift the blame onto someone else.

10. "Out came this calf!" is descriptive of the effrontery, folly, and unreasonableness of excuses and should move us to see how foolish we sound when we make excuses.

11. No sin is self-contained. It affects the individual who commits it. It draws others into its evil and its consequences. It rises as a stench to the nostrils of God and dis-

honors Him. Thus, the rationalization "It's my life, I'll do with it what I want" proves to be senseless, ill-advised, and tragic.

12. The Levites were set apart to be caretakers of the tabernacle and aides to the priests. They were to have a special place in Israel as the tribe God claimed as uniquely His own and who had been chosen to serve the Lord in caring for that place where the Lord would meet His people.

13. Jesus expects us to love Him with a love greater than we have for our immediate family. Jesus is not saying that parents and family should not be loved by His disciples, but that He must come first in His disciples' lives, to be loved even more than one's family. The Levites' action should be judged in the light of their wholehearted and loyal response to God, not for its apparently coldhearted killing of "brother and friend and neighbor." The "brother and friend and neighbor" had displaced God with the golden calf and, therefore, were to be punished. Ultimately, in time and eternity, one's relationship to God alone is all that matters.

Day 4 • Exodus 32:31–33:11

14. (a) The righteous are listed in God's book of life. God blots out the names of those who are guilty of unrepented sin. (b) At the judgment the book of life (and other books containing the record of our lives on earth) will be opened; those whose names are not written in the book of life will be consigned to hell. (c) Only those whose names are written in the book of life will be admitted to heaven.

15. (a) God holds the guilty responsible for their own sins; no one will be held responsible for the sins of another. (b) While it is true that no one can pay for the sins of another because no one is righteous enough to make sufficient and satisfactory atonement for his or her own sins, let alone for someone else's, the Gospel promise is that in Jesus Christ there is one without sin who has become the propitiation for all sin—credited to the individual if Christ's payment is accepted as God's gift, by faith.

16. "Now go, lead the people" is Moses' assurance that God, despite His fierce anger and threatened punishments, would relent and continue His covenant with Israel, fulfilling His promise to bring them to the land "flowing with milk and honey" (Exodus 33:3).

17. God wants us to express our repentance by acknowledging and confessing our sin so that we might receive forgiveness and by earnestly desiring to amend our sinful ways.

18. To other prophets the Lord revealed Himself through visions, dreams, and other indirect means. But with Moses the Lord spoke directly and personally.

Day 5 • Exodus 33:12–23

19. (a) Moses argued that if the Presence of the Lord did not accompany Israel to the Promised Land, how would other nations know that God had chosen them as His kingdom of priests and His own treasured possession? How would they know that God had chosen Moses to lead this people? (b) We have been baptized and bear the name of Christ. We believe and proclaim the Gospel as God's gracious message of forgiveness for all who will receive this message and trust in the Savior God has given us.

20. **Challenge question.** As we consider Moses a forerunner of Christ, we may note that both were of obscure birth. Both were in great danger during infancy. Both lived their youth and early adulthood in obscurity. Both felt they had a mission but were rejected by family members. Both gave signs and miracles proclaiming their God-given mission. Both were law-givers; the law given through Moses was impossible for sinners to keep, but Jesus fulfilled that law for us and gave us the law of love. Both were founders of a new community. Both were great intercessors and teachers. Both were willing to be sacrificed for the sake of others, but only Jesus Christ was sacrificed and drew all people to Himself (John 12:32).

21. (a) Moses asked the Lord to show him His glory. The Lord replied that this request could not be granted, since any sinner who saw God's glory would die. (b) Nevertheless, although Moses could not see God's glory directly, the Lord would allow Moses to see His "back"—Moses would see God's glory indirectly, a reflection of His glory. (c) Believers see God's glory in His Son, Jesus Christ. That glory is seen by believers in this life through faith; in heaven, where we will be free of sin, we will see God's "face"—His full glory (Revelation 22:4).

The Renewal of the Covenant

Exodus 34

Preparing for the Session

Central Focus

This session concerns God's renewal of the broken covenant. It will focus especially on the revelation of God's nature and character.

Objectives

That the participant will be led to

1. repent of his or her rebellious sinful nature;
2. believe in the forgiveness that comes from God's graciousness;
3. rejoice in God's grace and compassion;
4. wholeheartedly love and trust in the Lord above all.

For the Small-Group Leader

In this lesson we are led once again from the darkness of Israel's apostasy into the radiance of God's presence. That occurred for Israel because in Moses they had an intercessor who was able to approach God on their behalf from the favored position in which God had put him. We may pass through the darkness of our own rupturings of God's covenant and experience renewal and enter again the brightness of His compassion and mercy. We, too, have an intercessor—Jesus Christ.

Watch, then, for two points of focus in this lesson: the humility and strength with which Moses interceded for Israel before the Lord and the radiancy Moses carried back to the people because of his face-to-face relationship with God. Moses shows the genuine happiness in a relationship with God that flows from a humble and contrite spirit. The second focus helps us to see our own radiant lives as reflections of God's glory. This focus should help us see God as much more than the chief character of the Bible, but to know Him fully as the real presence in our own lives.

Small-Group Discussion Helps

Day 1 • Exodus 34:1–7

1. Though broken, God's covenant with Israel had been restored and was just as it had been before. God does not forgive partially or conditionally but completely and unconditionally.

2. We do not expect the Lord to appear to us in a visible or glorious manner until He comes again in His glory at the end of the age. Nevertheless, we do recognize and feel God's presence among us at various times. Many feel the reality of God's presence when receiving Holy Communion or during Sunday worship. Others may feel the Lord's presence particularly during periods of prayer or meditation. Encourage participants to share when they have occasionally or usually do feel the presence of the Lord in a special way.

3. (a) In contrast to the medieval church, the Puritans, and legalistic sects, where God is pictured as condemning and wrathful, many would say that God's image among us today has gone to the other end of the spectrum, emphasizing God's compassion to the exclusion of His threatened punishment. Such an emphasis tends to put aside human responsibility for meeting God's standards. It often also leads to a caricature of God as a permissive "wimp" who excuses sin, rather than the holy God who condemns sin but forgives sinners for Jesus' sake. (b) We must not fail to remember the clear description of Scripture, as here in 34:6–7, that God is holy and just and requires obedience, as well as being the compassionate and merciful God who is love. Forgetting that God is the God of justice plays down the seriousness of sin and does away with the necessity of Jesus' cross to make atonement for sin, while forgetting that God is the God of mercy makes our situation hopeless. Both distortions rob us of the Gospel by denying its need on the one hand or its reality on the other.

4. We find quite a list of God's attributes, or characteristic qualities, in Exodus 34:6–7: compassion, grace, patience, love, faithfulness, forgiveness, and justice.

5. (a) The Ezekiel text clearly points out that individuals are punished for their own sin, not that of their parents. (b) Deuteronomy 7:9 tells us that the Lord's faithfulness extends "to a thousand generations of those who love Him and keep His commands." Exodus 34:7 tells us that the Lord punishes the sins of the fathers to the third and fourth generation. (Exodus 20:5 adds "of those who hate Me," making it clear that the Lord does not punish believing children for the sins of unbelieving fathers.) A comparison of these two verses indicates that God's grace far exceeds His just punishment.

Day 2 • Exodus 34:8–10

6. (a) Moses approaches God humbly. He bows before the Lord, indicating total submissiveness to Him. He reminds God of His promises even as he expresses no special worthiness for God to fulfill His promises. He frankly acknowledges the people's stubbornness and resulting sin. Then, and only then, does he ask God to continue His relationship with Israel. (b) Our own prayers to the Lord need these characteristics of awe and respect, humility and confession.

7. God's promise in giving the covenant for the second time has a futuristic tone: He "will do wonders never before done" (34:10).

Day 3 • Exodus 34:11–17

8. If love means anything at all, it means trust. In marriage, mutual trust must exist if there is mutual love. Defining jealousy positively, we build our love on trust and our trust on jealousy, acknowledging that our "other self" has every right to expect our faithfulness.

9. Common to pagan religions were the fertility cults leading to sexual excesses and immorality. Devotion to Asherah and El displayed sexual immorality in cultic observances. For Israel such devotion displayed the most serious unfaithfulness to God Himself. Participation in rites that worshiped and looked to Asherah for blessing was unfaithfulness to God, just as looking to another person for the love we should look for in our spouse constitutes unfaithfulness in marriage.

10. Paul draws a comparison of the love existing between husband and wife to the love existing between the Lord and His church. Christ is the head of the church, and the husband is the head (leader) of the wife in marriage. The church willingly and in love submits to Christ, and the wife is to willingly and in love submit to her husband. Christ loved the church and gave His life for its redemption. Husbands are to love their wives and devote their lives to the welfare of their wives. The church is the body of Christ, and husbands are to regard their wives as part of themselves and to devote the care and concern for their wives as they would to their own bodies. Christ and the church are one; husbands and wives are one.

11. This is meant to be a thought-provoking question that will lead us to see again how important it is to be the sort of Christian who has the Bible in one hand and the newspaper in the other, analyzing our world with the direction God's Word gives us. Would you agree (and can you support your agreement with examples) that a weakening of faith in God—varying from total unbelief to indifference to accommodation of God's Word with personal desires—runs parallel to the adulteration and fornication of our human sexuality? If God is dismissed, considered unimportant, or manipulated to one's satisfaction, will not His will expressed in the Ten Commandments suffer the same fate?

12. (a) Paul urges believers not to be "yoked together," joined in a close and lasting relationship, with unbelievers. Though not specifically addressed to marriage, it would be hard to find a relationship that better fits Paul's meaning. (In 1 Corinthians 7:39 Paul counsels marriageable Christian women to marry a man who is also a believer.) (b) A common Christian faith has obvious advantages to a couple. They would share mutual values and goals. They would have a strong commitment in their love. Their Christian faith would teach them forgiveness and consideration toward each other. Other advantages will also come to mind. (c) On the other hand, the lack of such advantages will deprive a marriage of a common base, perhaps of common values and goals, and common experiences of an important nature. This is not to say, however, that such a marriage will be unsuccessful. Success, however, will be more difficult. (d) Paul encourages a Christian married to an unbeliever to remain loyal and faithful and to sanctify the marriage and family by prayer and a holy life that will commend the Christian faith to the unbelieving spouse and to other family members. Peter gives similar counsel. In fact, the Christian partner

is to be especially concerned to set an example of faith and faithfulness so that, if possible, he or she might win the spouse and family for the Lord.

Day 4 • Exodus 34:18–28

13. God rightfully claimed the first and the best of the yearly harvest from Israel. He was their God, and it was through His blessing that the harvest came. Everything we are and have comes from and belongs to the Lord. We are stewards, or trustees, of these things. While this ritual stipulation refers to the "firstfruits of the harvest of your soil" (34:26), we may surely apply the general stewardship principle to ourselves: we offer back to God the firstfruits of our own labor, usually in the form of monetary offerings during a service of worship.

14. The Lord was concerned to protect the Israelites from the religion they would find among the Canaanites. The religion of these people was particularly immoral, coarse, and cruel. It appealed to the worst in people and so would be a particularly potent threat to the Israelites.

Day 5 • Exodus 34:29–35

15. The radiant face of Moses must be explained as a reflection of God's glory.

16. **Challenge question.** Essentially Paul's argument is this: (a) If the Old Covenant "that brought death" could bring such glory into peoples' lives, how much more the New Covenant that brings life! (b) Paul carries his argument another step. A veil covers the faces of those who do not see the glory of God in the New Covenant expressed in Jesus Christ. But when one, like Moses, sees the glory of God in Jesus Christ, the veil is removed and (c) we will reflect "the Lord's glory" (2 Corinthians 3:18).

17. (a) Moses was unaware of the radiance that was revealed in his appearance. This points to Moses' humility and unassuming nature—a characteristic explicitly referred to in Numbers 12:3. (b) As we concentrate more on Christ and on our reasons to love and thank Him, we will become less self-conscious and less self-glorifying in our service as God's people.

18. Is it possible for us to overwhelm people with our genuinely good lives? People might shy away from sincere and earnest Christians because they feel the implicit judgment of their own lives by the comparison. (See, for example, the reaction of Peter to Jesus in Luke 5:8.) But we are more likely to scare people away with a self-righteousness that is pharisaical. (See Jesus' description of the Pharisee and the tax collector, Luke 18:9–14.)

19. We can only imagine what Moses said as he "called to them." We are probably not far from the truth when we hear in that call—which is also ours—the call of Christ, which supports and comforts, guides and strengthens (Matthew 11:28–30). Words and actions spoken and done in Christ's love will be more readily understood and appreciated.

The Building of the Tabernacle

Exodus 35–40

Preparing for the Session

Central Focus

This session is based on chapters 35–40, which report how the tabernacle complex was made and erected. Special attention will be given to the significance of the overall layout, to the Lord's tabernacling presence, and to God's people as a pilgrim people.

Objectives

That the participant will be led to

1. acknowledge the unholy and sinful nature of all people;
2. receive by faith the forgiveness and holiness Christ Jesus gives;
3. rejoice that the Lord graciously tabernacles with His people;
4. understand more fully what it means to be Christ's holy and pilgrim people;
5. dedicate his or her abilities and possessions in service to the Lord Jesus Christ by the power of the Holy Spirit working through the Gospel;
6. eagerly await the second advent of the Lord, when all space and time will be filled with His holiness.

Small-Group Discussion Helps

Day 1 • Exodus 35:1–29

1. Keeping the Sabbath as a day of rest and of reflection on God's work was a new way of life for the Israelites. God had not asked this of them before the giving of the Law at Sinai. No doubt repeated reminders were necessary until keeping the Sabbath became ingrained into their routine.

Furthermore, the Israelites were about to undertake with great enthusiasm an absorbing project—making the tabernacle and its furnishings. They would need to remember that keeping the Sabbath as God had commanded them was even more important than giving themselves enthusiastically to this project, as important as it was.

2. (a) The Lord God instructed Adam to work in the Garden of Eden before the fall into sin; work is not a consequence of sin—though the hardship and frustration often connected with work did result from sin. (b) To the Ephesians Paul wrote that Christians ought to work with their own hands, not only to provide their own necessities but also so they may have something to share with those in need who are unable to provide for themselves. (c) Paul encouraged the Colossians to do everything (including their work) in the name of the Lord Jesus, with a thankful heart toward God. (d) Paul admonished the Thessalonian Christians not only to be busy themselves but even to avoid those who are idle. He cites his own example. (Paul earned his living as a tentmaker, Acts 18:2–3.) Paul laid down this rule for the Thessalonians: "If a man will not work, he shall not eat."

3. While the preservation of life and health certainly require immediate attention, participants will be able to suggest many things that often interfere with worship that ought not—recreation and pleasure-oriented activities, work of an optional nature or work that might be postponed, unnecessary travel, visiting that could be done another time, and so forth.

4. Not only do our bodies and minds need rest each week, but our souls need the rest, refreshment, and recreation provided by worship.

5. God-pleasing stewardship springs from a desire to serve God and to honor and praise Him. We know this is our responsibility, and we are glad to do it. Our stewardship also advances God's kingdom and provides for the needs of others, starting with their need to hear the Gospel. God-pleasing stewardship is voluntary and cheerfully done.

Day 2 • Exodus 35:30–36:38

6. Paul tells us that the gifts of the Spirit are to be used for the common good and not only for our own profit or advantage. In effect, spiritual gifts belong to the whole church and not only to those to whom they are entrusted.

7. (a) The Lord provides the church and Christians individually with what is needed to do His work and will. God will not give people responsibilities for which He has not provided the resources to fulfill those responsibilities. (b) We are to respond wholeheartedly to the tasks the Lord sets before us, confident that He has given what is necessary for their accomplishment. We are to be busy at these tasks continually, until the Lord Himself shows us that the task is completed and we may stop.

8. (a) Both the Israelites and the Macedonians gave gladly and sacrificially, beyond what might have been expected. (b) Paul explains the motivation and power behind this remarkable generosity when he tells us that Macedonians "gave themselves first to the Lord and then to us in keeping with God's will." (c) If we should begin to feel that the Lord is asking too much of us by asking us to be generous, we need only remember that Jesus Himself, "though He was rich, yet for your sakes He became poor, so that you through His poverty might become rich" (2 Corinthians 8:9) and that God's "indescribable gift" to us is the gift of salvation and eternal life. This helps us see our own generosity in a proper perspective.

Day 3 • Exodus 37–38

9. Jesus reversed the practice of the world, which makes honor by others the mark of success and achievement. Instead, the Christian is a successful achiever when serving others selflessly and without recognition. Jesus Himself models the attitude He would instill in us, His followers. One motivation should drive our Christian service: glamorous or unglamorous, we do it in the Lord's name, to God's glory, for Christ's sake.

10. Ultimately, all of Scripture is related in some way to God's overall goal for His Word. God inspired Scripture so that it might teach us how we might be saved through faith in Jesus. This is the primary goal of the Bible. Other goals, which support the primary goal, are that Christians might be taught, rebuked, corrected, and trained in godly living.

Day 4 • Exodus 39

11. Most all of us know the human inclination to "get by." That's why we should be honest in evaluating the time, ability, and money we give to the Lord's work. Is it, indeed, the best we can do? Whether teaching in the Sunday school, keeping church financial records, serving on administrative committees or boards, or helping to clean or maintain buildings or grounds, we will want to do the very best of which we are capable.

12. Constructing the tabernacle and its furnishings was a project that had the very highest priority, since God Himself had provided the pattern for how it was to be made. In this structure the Lord would meet His people with His grace. No more important structure can be imagined than this tabernacle. Certainly, then, Moses inspected the work to ensure that it met its divinely given specifications.

13. It is significant to note the order of Moses' reaction to the Israelites' accomplishment. First came the inspection; then the blessing. We might bless those who do well in serving the Lord (a) by thanking God for service well done and for the faithful servants who did it, as Paul thanked God for the Philippians. That prayer of thanksgiving might be spoken privately or in public. Paul wrote publicly of the prayers he spoke privately. (b) Paul also thanked and commended the Philippians and told them how their generous gift was an offering that was pleasing to God. (c) We might thank people in various ways, with a personal word, with a public acknowledgment, even with a gift or other tangible expression of gratitude.

Day 5 • Exodus 40

14. Commemoration of milestones are common throughout Scripture. The tabernacle would be an important fixture in the Old Testament; it would serve as the meeting ground between Israel and the Lord until the days of King Solomon, some 450 years later. Furthermore, the plan and furnishings of the tabernacle would be replicated in the temples that followed it. Most important, the tabernacle was a visible sign and means of God's gracious presence with His people, and it emphasized the importance of worship.

15. (a) "Holy" means to be set apart for God's purpose. That was accomplished by the consecration of the taber-

nacle, of its furnishings, and of the priests who served in it. This consecration was done by the use of the anointing oil. (b) The Hebrew word for anointing is the word from which comes the term *Messiah.* The anointing of the tabernacle and its priesthood looked ahead to the coming of Jesus, the Messiah, who was anointed with the Holy Spirit to fulfill God's plan to save us and the entire world from sin and death. (c) Answers will vary but will no doubt share the joy we have in knowing that we belong to God and have His Spirit as our empowering helper in our new life in Christ.

16. God's glory was usually made visible by a heavenly brightness or brilliance. Now God's glory is hidden from earthly eyes. Believers see the glory of God in Christ and the Gospel through faith. But when Jesus returns again at the end of this age, all eyes will see His glory, and we believers will share in that heavenly glory!

17. Deuteronomy 34 concludes the story that Exodus begins. There we find that (a) Moses was not permitted to enter the Promised Land, though he was permitted to view it before he died. (b) The Lord Himself buried Moses' body in Moab, in the valley opposite Beth Peor, though the exact location was not disclosed. (c) Joshua the son of Nun was called by God to be Moses' successor.

18. This course concludes the study of Exodus. In the first course we saw how God called and redeemed His people, Israel, from Egypt. Our study of this second half of Exodus, hopefully, has made God's covenant with us and His dwelling with us not only more understandable, but, most of all, experientially real in the lives of all of those who have been part of your discussion group.